A PARENT'S GUIDE TO 1ST GRADE

▼

A PARENT'S GUIDE TO 1ST GRADE

HOW TO ENSURE YOUR CHILD'S SUCCESS

Peter W. Cookson, Jr., Ph.D. and Susan A. Mescavage, Ed. M.
Teachers College, Columbia University

With Joshua Halberstam, Ph.D. and Audra Watson

LEARNINGEXPRESS

NEW YORK

Copyright © 2000 LearningExpress, LLC.

Library of Congress Cataloging-in-Publication Data

Cookson, Peter W.
   A parent's guide to first grade : how to ensure your child's success / Peter W.
Cookson, Jr., and Susan A. Mescavage with Joshua Halberstam and Audra
Watson.—1st ed.
      p. cm.
   Includes bibliographical references.
   ISBN 1-57685-310-1 (pbk.)
   1. First grade (Education)—United States—Guidebooks. 2. Education,
Primary—Parent participation—United States—Guidebooks. 3. Parent-teacher
relationships—Guidebooks. I. Mescavage, Susan A. II. Title.

LB1571 1st .C66 2000
372.24'1—dc21   00-032719

All rights reserved under International and Pan-American Copyright Conventions. Published in the
United States by Learning Express, LLC, New York.
Reprinted materials:
Copyright © 2000 Lightspan, Inc., www.lightspan.com All rights reserved. See pages 24-25 and 28.
Copyright © 2000 Bell South Corportation. All rights reserved. See page 126.

Printed in the United States of America
9 8 7 6 5 4 3 2 1
First Edition

ISBN 1-57685-310-1

For more information or to place an order, contact LearningExpress at:

900 Broadway
Suite 604
New York, NY 10003

Or visit our website at:

www.LearnX.com

Acknowledgments

▼

With special thanks to Colleen Connors, formerly of LearningExpress, for researching her way through social skills and writing about extracurricular activities.

Katie Embree, Associate Director at the Center for Educational Outreach and Innovation at Teachers College, for her magical touch with moving this project along and keeping everyone in good spirits with her wonderful humor.

We'd also like to extend special thanks to Audra Watson, whose research, writing, and commitment to this book were extraordinary.

Contents

A Parent's Guide to 1st Grade

1

Welcome to First Grade

▼

WHERE YOU WILL FIND:

➤ A Welcome to First Grade
➤ A Look at Some Kindergarten Highlights
➤ A Brief Summary of Academic and Social Goals of First Grade
➤ An Outline of Your Role
➤ You and Your Child's Teacher
➤ How to Use This Book
➤ Some Items You Might Expect to See

First grade... an exciting year for you and your child. Not only is it the official start of the twelve-year journey through elementary, middle, and high school, but it's also a year full of changes and new challenges. First graders will learn to follow directions, pay attention for up to twenty minutes at a time, and tackle a schedule full of new and exciting subjects like reading, math, social studies, and science. Also, for many five- and six-year-olds, first grade will be their first all-day school experience.

Believe it or not, you have been your child's first, and possibly only, teacher until now. Congratulations on all your hard work! Your role as a parent-teacher has paved the way to first grade, the first year in a lifetime of learning.

It is important to know that your role is not finished. Simply by reading this book, you have proven your interest in what and how your child is learning. That is critical. Parental involvement is critical to your child's success in school and in life. You know your child best, so make the best of that knowledge.

As a parent, you want to get your child off to a positive start: to learn new things, adjust to a full day of learning, and have lots of new friends. The key is to know what will be expected of your child—both academically and socially—and how you can prepare her ahead of time and then support her once she's there. This book will provide some samples of the best ways to help you and your child make the most of the first grade experience.

A LOOK BACK

They say you can't know where you are going until you know where you have been.

In order to know what first grade has in store, let's look back on what was covered in kindergarten.

While not as rigorous as first grade, kindergarten covered several topics that your child will revisit in the years to come. The following are five topics that were covered in Reading/Language Arts:

➤ Listen to and follow instructions
➤ Know the letters of the alphabet
➤ Identify the first letter in a word
➤ Hold a pencil properly
➤ Make a connection between spoken and written language

The term *mathematics* is used loosely when discussing kindergarten. There were some topics covered in order to familiarize your child with math lessons to come.

➤ Identify and count numbers zero through ten
➤ Know by name the four basic shapes (circle, square, triangle, rectangle)
➤ Determine the difference between alike and different
➤ Sort objects with similar attributes
➤ Recognize the function of a calendar

Basically, while kindergarten was a time to learn how to go to school, first grade is your child's first step toward learning how to be a student.

FIRST GRADE ACADEMIC GOALS

The goal for your child in first grade will be to build on these skills and develop the fundamentals that will allow her to read, write, and complete simple math computations. Along with these skills, first grade will mark the first time your child will have writing, science, social studies, art, music, and possibly even computers as formal subjects. This may seem like a drastic step in the complexity of your child's education.

FIRST GRADE SOCIAL GOALS

First grade will also incorporate many of the social skills your child learned as a kindergartener. Children, especially only children, grow accustomed to having the undivided attention of their parents. In kindergarten, they have undoubtedly encountered the novel concepts of sharing, taking turns, and getting along with others, sometimes up to thirty others! Your first grader will be more accustomed to having classmates, so lessons in social skills will focus on responsibility, manners, and self-respect.

YOUR ROLE IN ALL OF THIS...

So what is your role in all of this? Well, as I am sure you know, your role is far from over. Your child will turn to you for guid-

> 66 Education is not the filling of a pail, but the lighting of a fire. 99
> — WILLIAM BUTLER YEATS

ance, help, support, and lots of positive reinforcement of the skills she is acquiring this year. For this reason, being educated about what she is doing and learning is going to better prepare you to help out in the most effective way.

Goals for First Grade Parents

There are many ways that a caring parent can ease the transition between kindergarten and first grade. Here are three goals that will help you to prepare your child ahead of time for this difficult transition. If you work toward these goals together, it will also serve as a support system for your child once he is in the classroom.

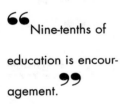

66 Nine-tenths of education is encouragement. **99**

— ANATOLE FRANCE

Ways to Prepare Your Child for the First Grade:

> ➤ **Talk about the first grade.** Familiarize your child with what's going to happen in the first grade. Use easy to understand language and give your child lots of time to ask questions. Sometimes just talking about an upcoming change helps ease anxiety and tension.
> ➤ **Master the alphabet and vowel sounds.** Make sure your child recognizes and knows the sounds of the ABCs before the first day of school. Practice every day until he has mastered them.

➤ **Develop math skills.** It's important that your child have a solid foundation with numbers, adding and subtracting, and problem solving skills. Use real-life opportunities in the kitchen, backyard, or on errands to figure out mathematical problems up to the number twenty.

Common Pitfalls to Watch For

As we've been discussing, first grade involves making a dramatic transition from kindergarten. Even with the most diligent and committed parents, some kids still have difficulty making the transition to a full-day classroom, complete with rules and assignments. There are many new expectations placed on children, and some kids may have trouble keeping up. For instance, first graders are expected to do things on their own. In kindergarten, the teacher may have been more nurturing and accepting of dependence. However, first grade is serious business. Children should be able to work independently and make good decisions in social situations. The truth is, some children just are not developmentally ready for this challenge.

Some common traits that your child may have include:

➤ **Tiredness.** If your child was in a half-day kindergarten classroom, chances are he'll be very tired at the end of a full-day schedule.
➤ **Nervousness.** Beginning the first grade is a scary experience. You should expect some nervousness and apprehension about the process.
➤ **Forgetfulness.** Most six- and seven-year-olds are a bit absentminded, leaving things at home and at school.

More serious obstacles include:

➤ Crying easily and often
➤ Dreading going to school
➤ Frustration with learning to read or reading below grade level
➤ Unable to work independently
➤ Aggressiveness
➤ Trouble staying on task long enough to finish an assignment

> 66 It is important for learning that a child be emotionally available. 99
>
> —ANNETTE BRODY, ST. LUKE'S SCHOOL

Parents and families can help first grade children avoid these pitfalls and sail straight into academic and social success by working closely with the classroom teacher to identify potential problems and find solutions. The key is to recognize the importance of becoming an active partner in your child's schooling. If you're a part of the schooling process, chances are you'll be quick to spot trouble and fix it. This active parenting will result in a more successful first grade experience for your child.

PARENTS AND TEACHERS

Parents need to recognize that teachers have the best interest of the children in mind. For this reason, parents should welcome the opportunity to develop a lasting and healthy partnership with their child's teacher. Children will view their teacher as an authority figure, as they would their own parents, but children should be taught to appreciate the teacher as someone who wants to help. Parents need to explain to their children that a teacher is not someone to be feared, but someone to be respected. After all, would you want to create the impression that the teacher is a dictator and then expect your child to look forward to spending seven hours a day with her? The answer is no.

A great way to establish a strong relationship with your child is to get to know your child's teacher. Here are a few helpful ways to developing a partnership with your child's teacher.

> ➤ Keep in regular contact with your child's teacher to insure that no major difficulties arise
> ➤ Discuss your expectations for your child's education
> ➤ Make a checklist of things that you think are important for your child to learn; does it match with the teacher's priorities?

Parents and Children: The First Grade Partnership

First grade can be a rewarding and special time for you to spend together. It doesn't take long for kids to notice that mom and dad are interested in their schoolwork and are committed to their success. Helping them in whatever way you can is a building block to future success. This is a wonderful way to shower your children with attention, love, and support. Chances are, the partnership you have with your child will help him do well in school, develop a pos-

> **"**Education is too important to be left solely to the educators.**"**
>
> —FRANCIS KEPPEL

itive self-image, and be well on his way to developing into a responsible adult. This book will guide you into becoming a supportive and knowledgeable first grade parent. Before long, first grade will be a fun, exciting, and rewarding experience for *everyone*.

Remember that:

> ➤ It's OK if your child is not yet reading. There's plenty of time to develop that skill throughout the school year.
> ➤ Some children find the transition to a full day packed with learning and rules to be difficult. Before long, they'll fall into the routine of first grade. Wait and see!
> ➤ Spending time with your child doing homework together is not only helping your child, but it's also a rewarding experience for you.

HOW TO USE THIS BOOK

This book is a compilation of facts that will allow you to know more about your child and how to help your child become a happy and well-educated person. Each chapter covers a different topic that parents can use as a reference for information as well as a resource for ideas. This is not meant to be comprehensive. As aforementioned, you know your child best. Instead, use this book to be part of your child's new life in the world of elementary school.

> 66 Better education is everybody's business. 99
>
> —U.S. Secretary of Education, Richard W. Riley

At Home Reading Log

▼

WEEK OF:

DAY	NAME OF BOOK AND PAGES OR CHAPTER READ
Monday	
Tuesday	
Wednesday	
Thursday	
Friday	

PARENT'S SIGNATURE: _____

As your child starts to read, chances are the teacher will encourage the keeping of a reading log to track how much and how often your child is reading. This is an ideal item to keep on the refrigerator so that you can both be proud of the work being done.

Sample Handwriting Practice

▼

Chapter 2 will outline the lessons to be taught regarding handwriting and penmanship. So that your child can develop good penmanship, sheets such as this will be used to practice.

First Grade Math Worksheet

Directions: Add the two numbers to find the sum of each problem.

9	6	7	7	5
+4	+3	+5	+6	+3
___	___	___	___	___

4	7	7	7	5
+2	+1	+1	+5	+2
___	___	___	___	___

4	5	9	9	9
+3	+1	+6	+8	+3
___	___	___	___	___

10	2	10	5	10
+8	+1	+9	+4	+2
___	___	___	___	___

7	4	4	3	3
+5	+1	+2	+1	+2
___	___	___	___	___

Although teachers always try to make math more interesting, standard worksheets such as this are common for first graders so that they can practice their basic skills.

The Days of the Week

▼

One day before Friday is _____

One day after Thursday is _____

Two days before Sunday is _____

Four days after Saturday is _____

Five days before Thursday is _____

Children sometimes have difficulties explaining and understanding time. A worksheet like the one featured here will help them with math and with the days of the week.

Colors

▼

COLOR	ITEM THAT IS THIS COLOR

Children will need to know all the colors of the rainbow, and this worksheet will help them. Children will also learn how to relate their knowledge of colors to the world around them.

Spelling List

▼

the

and

but

see

like

with

come

as

what

to

Children in first grade are just learning to spell. For this reason, spelling lists will tend to focus on the basics.

2

What Your Child Is
Learning in School...

▼

CURRENT MOVEMENT: STANDARDS

It's tough to pinpoint exactly what your first grader is learning in school. Each state, from Hawaii to Maine, has its own opinions about what its students should learn and know. In an effort to increase the academic achievement of students, states throughout the country are undertaking self-studies as to what they think each grade from kindergarten through high school should teach. The results of these studies are *standards*. Standards are simply what states expect students to know in each subject in grade levels from kindergarten through high school. The key question for states is this: "How good is good enough?" In other words, state departments of education, together with other learning organizations, try to define what a child should know and how she should be able to demonstrate that learning. In educational "talk," these are referred to as *content standards* and *performance standards*. These are simply what will be taught to your child and how he will show that he has learned it.

It is important to know what these standards are. If you and your child know what is expected, you can avoid much of the anxiety that comes with schooling. Your child's school or district office will have this information. It is simply a matter of requesting it. Or, if you have access to the Internet, most states' departments of education have websites that outline and explain their specific learning standards. Check out *www.homeworkcentral.com* for a listing of each state's websites.

Go to: www.homeworkcentral.com

Click on "Parent"

Click on "Parents and Schools"

Click on "National Education Standards"

WHAT CHILDREN ARE LEARNING IN FIRST GRADE:

There are certain subjects that are included in virtually all first grade curricula throughout the country. Below, you'll find a list of these tried-and-true subjects. An outline of the goals and content for each subject are included here so that you'll know what to expect and how you can help. The best way to become an involved parent is to understand what your child is expected to know and to do everything you can to make him successful in his schoolwork. So, get ready for a quick overview of the typical first grade curriculum. Typical first grade subjects are as follows:

The Core Subjects:
- ➤ Reading & Language Arts
- ➤ Writing
- ➤ Math
- ➤ Social Studies
- ➤ Science

The Other Subjects:
➤ Computer Lab
➤ Art
➤ Music
➤ Physical Education
➤ Safety

You've all scrambled out of the house in the morning and said your goodbyes at the bus stop or in front of the school, but then what? Perhaps you are like some parents who know as little about what their child's daily schedule is like as their child does about what they do at work all day. This chapter is designed to give you a sense of how your child spends her time and what she is supposed to get from her time at school.

This is a sample schedule of how your child might spend her day. This schedule was provided by Annette Brody, a teacher in New York.

Sample Schedule

8:30 A.M.	Meeting time (Pledge of Allegiance, attendance)
9:00 A.M.	Language Arts lesson (reading, discussion, writing activities, handwriting)
10:00 A.M.	Small group activities (skill instruction, independent work)
11:15 A.M.	Math
11:55 A.M.	Lunch/Recess
12:40 P.M.	Silent reading
1: 00 P.M.	Rotating subjects (Art, Music, Foreign language, or Computer lab)
1: 40 P.M.	Social Studies or Science
2:20 P.M.	Storytime
2:35 P.M.	Afternoon recess
3:00 P.M.	Dismissal

Because so many foundation skills in Language Arts are learned in second grade, fifty percent of your child's day will likely be spent in reading, writing, vocabulary, grammar, punctuation, speaking, listening, and literature. Mathematics occupies about thirty percent of the day. For this reason, schools offer a "rotating schedule."

Simply put, the other subjects such as Social Studies, Science, and Art are taught on alternating days. Educational standards require that second graders have 310 minutes (five hours) of instruction in the day.

A SYNOPSIS OF ALL SUBJECTS TAUGHT IN THE FIRST GRADE

Many parents may feel they know what their child is doing in school. After all, the three Rs (Reading, Writing, and Arithmetic) have been standards for generations. This chapter is going to list and describe the subjects your child is studying at school as standards (national and state) for what your child should know as a second grader. From national standards to sample curricula from schools across the United States, this will let you know how your child spends her day.

The core subjects that are being taught in every school are Reading/Language Arts, Writing, Math, Social Studies, and Science. While these subjects are invariable, there are a number of special subject areas that are taught depending on the location of the school and its resources. These special subjects include but are not limited to Music, Art, Computer Lab, Foreign Language, Safety and Physical Education. But what do these subject headings really mean? Read on to find out.

Reading/Language Arts

This subject heading may seem vague to parents and students alike. While children in the second grade are assumed to be reading at a level appropriate to their age, the emphasis in language arts focuses on the innovation behind the skill. Topics that fall under this category include reading, reading comprehension, listening and speaking, and grammar.

Writing: It's not just penmanship.

This subject is more self-explanatory. While penmanship is an area of focus in this subject, writing includes lessons that build skills in brainstorming ideas, organization, writing using reference materials, and descriptive words (e.g. Creative Writing). These topics are sometimes included in Language Arts, as the two subjects are interdisciplinary.

Math: It all adds up.

Arithmetic has remained a standard. In this subject, your child will work on addition, subtraction, multiplication, and division.

Social Studies

Subjects that fall under this broad category include History, Geography, Cultural Studies, and Current Events.

Science

This topic is intended to include studies from Life Science (e.g., animals, biology), Earth Science (e.g., rocks, volcanoes), and Natural History (e.g., dinosaurs).

Music

Topics will vary from school to school, provided that a school even has a designated curriculum that includes music. This area of study is meant to involve children in singing, playing an instrument, and responding to music.

Art

Again, many schools, due to lack of funding for staff and supplies, may not offer art as a standard part of the curriculum. Art classes can include developing visual art skills (painting, drawing, sculpting) as well as theater and dance classes.

Computer Lab

Students' accessibility to computers and the Internet is increasingly important as the use of computers dominates work, school, and home. Unfortunately, not all schools have sufficient funding for large networked computer labs.

Foreign Language

Spanish, French, and Latin are a few of the languages to which your child may be exposed this year.

Reading/Language Arts

Let's start with the most fundamental of all subjects in the first grade—Reading/Language Arts. Reading will open up and personalize the world of books to your first grader. Your child loves to be read to, so just imagine how much fun she'll have when she develops the skills to read to herself. By the time she's finished with first grade, she'll be able to read exciting adventures of all kinds of characters like astronauts and explorers, actually bringing her academic studies to life. A perfect example of this phenomenon is the early reader series *The Magic School Bus*. Children who read these books follow the adventures of Ms. Frizzle, a wacky and brilliant teacher, as she leads her students on expeditions full of discovery.

Reading is also the essential ingredient to understanding other subjects such as math. The ability to read the examples given in textbooks and worksheets will help build and develop vital math skills covered in the lessons as well as allow children to begin to solve word problems.

First and foremost, first grade is the time for *learning how to read*. All other subjects revolve around reading/language arts acquisition. By the time your child enters third grade, there will be a dramatic switch to *reading to learn*. Now is the time to develop those basic reading skills that will help your child be prepared for the challenges awaiting him in the later grades.

Goals of a First Grade Reading Program

The primary goal of the first grade Reading/Language Arts curriculum is for children to become *independent readers*. This does not mean that your six- or seven-year-old should be able to read any book in the library. What is does mean is that by the end of the first grade, your child should be able to read books appropriate to beginning readers. If you are uncertain if a certain book is appropriate for your child's developmental stage, simply look on the back of the book—most publishers print the target age group right on the back cover to make it easy to choose the right book.

How will your child reach this goal? Most children need a steady stream of TLC to stick with the challenge and become a *reader.* The best way for your child to get comfortable with reading is through a combination of solid instruction at school, support and encouragement at home, both reading aloud and being read to, and daily practice reading different types of books.

Some of the key components of a solid first grade reading program include:

➤ **Oral Language.** First graders will have numerous opportunities to develop oral language skills such as speaking and listening. One opportunity is through the reading aloud of quality literature. Also, children will be asked to talk about the books that have been read to them, and to ask questions and/or summarize what the story was about.

➤ **Phonemic Awareness.** Phonemic awareness is the understanding that individual sounds combine together to create words. Children—and adults, too—use phonemic awareness each time they try to "sound out" unfamiliar words. In the first grade, students will be taught phonemic awareness by the systematic instruction of letter sounds. This includes individual consonants, short vowels, long vowels, initial blends (st, tr, cl, fl, bl, gl, gr, sl, br), and digraphs (th, sh, ch, wh).

Another aspect of phonemic awareness is the ability to recognize patterns of words. First graders will be expected to decode one-syllable words following a consonant/vowel (CV) pattern such as *me, to,* and *be.* They will also need to decode consonant/vowel/consonant (CVC) words such as *cat, dog,* and *bat.* Finally, first graders need to know the consonant/vowel/consonant plus silent e pattern. Examples of this pattern are *kite* and *bone.*

Your child's teacher may use phonetically-controlled reading material to help your child experience the sounds, blends, or word patterns being taught. You probably remember the *Sam Sat on the Hat* type of books from your younger days. Predictable books such as these use simple stories with small vocabulary words to teach decoding skills within a natural context. With direct instruction and practice, it won't be long before your child can read the story himself.

➤ **Comprehension Skills.** Aside from the technical aspects of reading, first graders learn basic comprehension skills to decipher the meaning of books. They will be expected to respond to **who, what, when, where,** and **how** questions. Specific skills include recalling details, following directions, sequencing events, determining main ideas, making inferences, anticipating meaning, and predicting events.

➤ **Sight Words.** There are a large number of "sight words" that occur very often in reading. They can be tricky because they often do not conform to the usual letter-sound patterns. Most first grade programs will teach common sight words such as *the, an, said, come, give* and *of* and drill the children with flash cards. The Dolch List of Sight Words compiles over 200 of the most common sight words in the English language. Learning these words is a great step for your child to take to become an independent reader. For a complete list of sight words, go to *http://library.thinkquest.org/50027/TeacherParents/Sight WordsList.html.*

Whole Language vs. Phonics Debate

You've probably heard rumblings of the debate between whole language and phonics. Phonics is simply one of the strategies readers use to sound out unfamiliar words. Whole language, on the other hand, is a set of beliefs about how children acquire language skills. Most first grade reading programs use the philosophy of whole language coupled with a systematic and organized instruction of phonics. This is referred to as a balanced literacy approach and is a win-win strategy to producing top-notch, independent first grade readers. If you are concerned about which approach your child's school is practicing, ask the teacher to explain more about the reading program to you. She'll be glad that you're interested. Or, for more information on whole Language, see www.familyplay.com/advice/mcmillan/e0604phonics.html or www.carolhurst.com/profsubjects/wholelanguagegetting.html

Writing

Children are born writers. We only need to think about crayon-covered walls for proof that kids like to write and draw. While you may not have been pleased at having to clean up the mess, your child was probably pleased with the proof of her writing skill. Schools try to tap into this enthusiasm from the moment your child enters kindergarten, when children begin to express themselves in written form.

Goals of a First Grade Writing Program

Just like reading, the goal of a first grade writing program is to produce *independent writers*. Because six- and seven-year-olds are just beginning writers, they will use pictures and simple words to express their thoughts, ideas, and feelings. These are the roots of learning how to write well.

That said, it's important to remember to be patient with developing writers. Focusing on misspellings can be discouraging, so your child's teacher will concentrate on the content and ideas expressed in your child's piece. Correcting every mistake on a child's written assignment actually does little for her writing ability and can squelch her enthusiasm for writing. Rest assured that lapses in spelling will be corrected during specific spelling drills in class.

Another goal of first grade writing programs is to help children learn to enjoy and value the writing process. Kids can't wait to tell their stories and share their ideas in both spoken and written form. At first, speedy delivery takes precedence over careful language usage. However, children want to write *right*. It's not long before they will focus on spelling, punctuation, and vocabulary themselves. But for right now, in the first grade classroom, these mechanics of writing will come with time, instruction, and practice. There's no need to rush.

Content

The first grade writing curriculum is focused on the basics, namely, learning to write letters and words and how to construct a sentence. Most first graders should be able to write two cohesive sentences about a picture or experience by the end of the first grade. Here are some of the nuts and bolts of a high-quality first grade writing program:

➤ **Writer's Workshop.** Many programs recognize the need for regular experiences with writing. Writer's workshops provide these experiences by devoting several periods a week just to the art of writing. Children are given the opportunity to make decisions about their writing, choose topics of interest, and develop their ideas creatively. Other key components of writer's workshops are student-teacher conferences, sharing with a friend, revising, editing, and publishing. This is a fabulous way to simulate the actual writing process and gives children a chance to understand the concept of beginnings, middles, and end of stories.

➤ **Opportunities to Write.** Children develop as writers when they have a variety of opportunities to share their thoughts and experiences. Classroom activities will offer your child a choice of topics that spark her enthusiasm and interest in recording her ideas on paper. Some activities include: journal writing, reading logs, and creating math word problems. Once she realizes the excitement of writing, she'll be motivated to learn the mechanics that pull it all together.

➤ **The Mechanics of Writing.** A good first grade program will introduce a few basic rules that will help your child write complete sentences. The first rule is *the use of capital letters* to begin sentences and names. A second rule is the use of *end punctuation* including periods, question marks, and exclamation points. Other rules involve the use of *contractions* and *making words plural*. While first graders will not use these rules with perfect accuracy, they will come to understand that rules play an important role in the writing process.

➤ **Printing Practice.** Your first grader will practice and practice printing. By the end of the year, he'll be expected to write upper-case letters in manuscript, lower-case letters in manuscript, and be able to write a complete sentence in manuscript. (Usually, cursive is taught in the second grade.)

Reading/Language Arts and Writing Breakdown

One of the best websites we have found containing information that is relevant to the grade level of your child is *Lightspan.com*. The following bulleted list was developed by the experts at Lightspan to give parents a better idea of what their child is learning.

Beginning of the Year

➤ Recognize the letters of the alphabet
➤ Read grade-appropriate literature
➤ Use phonics to sound out words
➤ Recognize and clap out syllables
➤ Utilize beginning concepts of spelling and capitalization
➤ Use temporary spellings
➤ Recognize compound words

- ➤ Listen attentively
- ➤ Listen to gain information and to appreciate literature
- ➤ Write complete sentences
- ➤ Write about one topic

Middle of the Year
- ➤ Begin to write independently
- ➤ Read age appropriate books independently
- ➤ Write legibly
- ➤ Read words with familiar word families or patterns
- ➤ Utilize concepts of spelling, capitalization, and punctuation
- ➤ Recognize traditional rhymes
- ➤ Recognize traditional folk tales and fairy tales
- ➤ Sequence information when writing

End of the Year

- ➤ Write legibly, while becoming aware of size of writing
- ➤ Read aloud
- ➤ Write using correct verb forms
- ➤ Make words plural where appropriate when writing

Mathematics

As with reading and writing, math is a skill that we use in our daily lives. As adults, we use mathematical thinking all the time. We calculate how much money we need to withdraw from the cash machine, how much time it will take to do all of our errands, and how much to tip the waiter at our favorite restaurant. First graders are just beginning to learn the skills necessary to make the same types of decisions.

Traditionally, first grade children have been taught basic arithmetic skills. When you were in elementary school, the focus of the math curriculum was probably drilling and practicing addition and subtraction facts such as 3+5=8. Today's math curriculum is very different than that. Children are still expected to know the same basic facts, however, today children are expected to understand the *why* behind problem solving.

Today's math will emphasize mathematical thinking and guide your child along to really understand how math is used in everyday life.

Goals of a First Grade Math Program

One goal of first grade math is to lay a solid foundation with numbers, adding and subtracting, and problem-solving skills. First grade is the time when children will master adding and subtracting to twenty and be able to count by twos and fives to one hundred. The best way to achieve this goal is with practice, practice, and more practice! While the thought of memorizing facts may be unappealing to you, it's perfectly fine to encourage your child to memorize her adding and subtracting facts to twenty. This is an invaluable gift that will save her tons of time at the higher levels of math.

But, adding and subtracting are only the beginning of what's expected in the first grade. Today's math places much emphasis on mathematical thinking and problem solving. Children as young as first graders will be expected to understand the logic behind addition and subtraction problems. In a first grade classroom, it's not uncommon to hear a teacher ask a student, "Explain the problem to me using words." Teachers may also ask first graders to explain a problem visually. It is not uncommon to hear a teacher ask a student something like, "Draw a picture of each step Johnny had to take to figure out how many baskets Shaquille O'Neill made in the game." The overall goal of teaching mathematical thinking is to help students become creative problem solvers of real-life math problems, not just number crunchers.

A third important goal of first grade math is to help students feel comfortable and good about math. Children pick up on the anxieties of "not getting it" fairly easily, leaving them feeling frustrated and lacking in mathematical talent. Math should be a fun learning experience. The goal of the first grade classroom is to help children feel excited about solving math problems and confident enough to tackle even the toughest problems.

Content

Whether your school district uses "new math," "old math," or a combination of both, here are the basic elements that are usually found in a first grade math program:

➤ **Numbers to one hundred.** Your child will be expected to read and write numerals one to one hundred. She should be able to count orally and write by fives and tens to one hundred and count orally and write by twos to fifty.

➤ **Addition.** Your child should be able to add vertical or horizontal problems involving ones and tens without regrouping (carrying over or borrowing).Some examples of this are:

$$
\begin{array}{r}
3 \\
+\ 5 \\
\hline
8
\end{array}
\qquad
3+5=8
\qquad
5+10=15
\qquad
\begin{array}{r}
5 \\
+10 \\
\hline
15
\end{array}
$$

She should also be able to add three addends with sums to twenty. Some examples include:

$$
\begin{array}{r}
4 \\
5 \\
+2 \\
\hline
11
\end{array}
\qquad
4+5+2=11
$$

➤ **Subtraction.** Your child should be able to subtract vertical or horizontal problems involving ones and tens without regrouping. Some examples of this are:

$$
\begin{array}{r}
4 \\
-2 \\
\hline
2
\end{array}
\qquad
5-2=3
$$

➤ **Word Problems.** First graders are expected to solve word problems using problem-solving strategies. They should also be able to illustrate or write about the steps needed to solve word problems.

➤ **Telling Time.** Your first grader will need to identify time to the hour and the half hour using traditional and digital clocks.

➤ **Money.** First graders are expected to give value to a group of pennies, nickels, dimes, quarters.

➤ **Calendar.** Your child should be able to use the calendar to identify the day and date. She should also be able to name the days of the week and understand the concepts of yesterday, today, and tomorrow.

➤ **Measurement.** First graders are expected to know how to use a ruler to measure to the inch. They should also be able to read simple bar graphs.

➤ **Geometry.** Your child should be able to identify and describe geometric figures: rectangles, squares, triangles, and circles. He should also be able to find the area of a figure by counting square units.

➤ **Statistics and Probability.** First graders should be able to interpret data in tables or graphs (picture, bar, circle, and line). They should also be able to collect, organize, and present data in tables or graphs (bar, circle, and line).

Math Breakdown

Again, the experts at Lightspan.com have compiled a comprehensive and grade specific list of what your child will be learning in math class this year.

Beginning of the Year

➤ Classify and sort objects by shape and color
➤ Skip count by twos, fives, and tens
➤ Recognize the seven days of the week by name and in order
➤ Identify equal parts

Middle of the Year

➤ Count forward and backward
➤ Recognize and apply the concepts of "greater than" and "less than"
➤ Recognize addition and subtraction facts zero to eighteen
➤ Add and subtract using one-digit numbers
➤ Identify number relationships
➤ Identify place value to the tens place
➤ Estimate length, capacity, and weight
➤ Recognize basic units of measure (inches, centimeters, cups, pounds, and degrees)
➤ Recognize the twelve months of the year by name and in order

End of the Year

➤ Count to one hundred or more by ones, fives, and tens
➤ Add and subtract two-digit numbers
➤ Recognize addition and subtraction facts zero to eighteen
➤ Recognize time in hours and half hours
➤ Identify A.M. and P.M.
➤ Understand the concept of time and recognize time on a clock face
➤ Identify the simple fractions ½, ⅓, and ¼
➤ Compare two or more graphs

Social Studies

Once first graders have mastered the basics of reading, writing, and math, they can use these skills to understand the world in which they live. Six- and seven-year-olds are naturally curious about the people, places, and things in their day-to-day lives. First grade offers children nearly seven hours of interaction with a social group other than their family. This opportunity presents new information about the world including differences in culture, food, lifestyle, and family makeup that may have been unknown before.

Social studies—put simply—is the study of people. It includes a look at how people live, work, get along with others, and solve problems. While some first grade classes limit their focus to lessons about family, neighborhood, and community, others broaden their scope to include a core of knowledge of world geography, world civilization, and history.

Goals of a First Grade Social Studies Program

The primary goal of first grade social studies is to learn the stories of different people and places. The study usually begins with lessons about the family, neighborhood, and community and later expands to historical stories about famous people, events, and places. These *history stories* bring facts, dates, and names to life for first graders. It is hoped that an early introduction to the value of history—whether it's personal or the story of others—will help students learn constructive social skills and become informed and responsible citizens. Luckily, first graders are naturally curious about the world. It's not difficult for teachers to tap into their active imaginations to make social studies fun and exciting for all.

Content

It's tough to determine precisely what your child will learn in social studies since it will vary from school to school. In some classrooms, it is a regular part of the curriculum; in others, it's something that's taught whenever there's extra time. There's even debate over what approach to take and which topics to teach. In short, there is not a national consensus about what a first grade social studies curriculum should look like. Here's a list of topics that we think are important parts of any first grade social studies program. If these topics are not taught at school, you can try them out as at-home projects.

➤ **Stories of ancestors.** Among the historical stories that first graders are likely to learn are the stories of the Ice Age and the ancient civilizations of Africa and Asia. They will also learn about world religions and peoples and begin a study of American geography and early American history. Your child will also be introduced to the time period, people, and places that existed between the Aztec and Mayan civilizations and the colonial period in America.

➤ **Social skills.** Another component of the first grade social studies curriculum is the development of social skills and responsibilities. A basic goal of first grade is to learn to work together, share, and cooperate. Social studies are a great way for children to learn and practice rules for participation as well as what their rights and responsibilities are as part of a group.

➤ **Historical literacy.** The first grade social studies curriculum will include the discussion of myths, legends, and biographies of outstanding women and men. In addition, children will also be given the opportunity to take on the roles of famous individuals and role-play what it was like to be that individual.

➤ **Geographic literacy.** This includes teaching an understanding of place, location, direction, and distance, as well as how to identify features in the environment. Maps and globes will also be introduced.

➤ **Adventure stories.** Your child's teacher is likely to heighten your child's curiosity by introducing him to adventure stories about families that crossed the oceans. These stories spark the imagination, as do stories about pioneers of the past and present.

➤ **Family structures.** Family life and structure and their variations may be studied. The roles of family members, variations in the way families live, interdependence of family members, and family life in earlier times in other cultures may also be studied.

Science

Children are scientists by nature. They are eager to explore the world around them and discover how things work and why things are the way they are. Real scientists work in much the same way. They ask questions, observe phenomena, and think about the discoveries they have made.

Science is an exciting, hands-on experience in which most children are thrilled to participate. However, many first grade classrooms—and other elementary grade levels, too—try to teach science through textbooks and worksheets, resulting in less-enthusiastic students. Children need to construct real experiments using water, ice, clay, food coloring, and steam. They need to write about their discoveries and use the skills of prediction and explanation to discover what's occurred. To really learn science well, children need hands-on opportunities to explore scientific concepts and practice the skills of scientific research.

Goals of a First Grade Science Program

A goal of first grade science is to provide children with real life experiences that foster the development of scientific thinking. What does scientific thinking involve? At the very basic level of science, there is a belief that through investigation, one can begin to understand the natural and physical world. Scientists observe, ask questions, gather and analyze data, and suggest explanations (scientists call them *theories*) that can be tested. This is known as *the scientific method.*

Children unknowingly use the scientific method when they encounter unknown things. Just think of a young toddler's reaction to a new toy. He will stare at it, pick it up, rattle it, put it in his mouth, and then usually figure out how it works. First graders have the same reaction to things they encounter every day such as water, ice, plants, animals, and heat. They will want to actively interact with these phenomena, just like the toddler with the rattle. The best thing first grade science curricula can do is to give them a chance to touch, taste, look, listen, and manipulate things to create explanations about how the world works.

Content

The content of first grade science will involve the development of science skills. These skills include:

➤ Asking questions
➤ Making predictions (scientists call them *hypotheses)*
➤ Conducting experiments
➤ Carefully observing
➤ Analyzing information and making conclusions
➤ Sharing the findings

These science skills are necessary to tackle the exploration of the world around us. They provide the logical, step-by-step approach that scientists use to go about explaining the unknown.

For first graders, science skills are especially helpful to explain the abstract concepts involved in the branches of science such as chemistry, biology, botany, and physics. Most first grade science curricula will have strands of earth science, life science, and physical science. Here is a brief glimpse at what you might find in first grade science class:

> **Living Things and Their Habitats.** Topics children might investigate include the forest habitat, the underground habitat, the desert habitat, and the water habitat. Other topics include the food chain, life cycles, and the behavior of birds, fish, insects, plants, or small animals.
> **Dinosaurs.** They may be extinct, but they are still hugely popular with the first grade set. Topics may include paleontologists, types of dinosaurs, and dinosaur habitats.
> **Oceans and Undersea Life.** Topics may include the oceans and tides, ocean currents, undersea life, and ways that humans interact with the oceans.
> **The Human Body.** First graders will be introduced to the major body systems including the skeletal, muscular, circulatory, digestive, and nervous systems. Related topics include germs and how to take care of their bodies.
> **Earth.** First graders will get an introduction to day and night, seasons, condensation and evaporation, climate and weather, land forms, recycling and garbage, and plants and soil.
> **Electricity and Energy.** Topics may include static electricity, the concept of on and off, conductors, safety rules, light, shadows, mirrors, rainbows, water, balls and ramps, magnets, and inventions.
> **Astronomy.** The solar system will be introduced in the first grade. Specific topics include the seven planets, the Moon, constellations, and Earth.

THE OTHER SUBJECTS

Computers

Ask any child, and they'll all tell you the same thing about computers—they're cool! Computers have a remarkable way of engaging even the most reluctant student. Whether it's educational games, word processing, or even pure playing, kids love being on a computer.

The good news for parents is that computers are powerful teaching tools and sources of information. Today's CD-ROMs and computer software bring learning to life for kids. They can also offer individualized instruction in a fun and exciting way. While the computer cannot replace a warm and caring teacher, it can offer students undivided attention and can tailor instruction to their skill levels, work pace, and learning styles. This is important for first graders who thrive on hands-on, active learning.

Content

Computers can play different roles in different schools. Some schools place great emphasis on encouraging computer skills, and their students spend substantial time on computers. Other schools don't because they lack the equipment, personnel, or facilities to do so. Whatever the case may be, here is a list of skills that we think are important for first graders to know:

- ➤ **Turning computers on and off.** First graders should know how to turn a computer on and how to safely turn it off.
- ➤ **Using a mouse.** Children need lots of experience manipulating a mouse to use it effectively.
- ➤ **Double-clicking.** Your child will need to know how to double click in order to save documents, open items, and exit programs. This is an easy-to-learn skill for most first graders because of their increased hand-eye coordination.
- ➤ **Opening programs.** It's important for second graders to be able to maneuver within a computer's hard drive to find their favorite programs and be able to open them up.
- ➤ **Basic typing skills.** First graders will need to have some familiarity with the keyboard to interact with word processing and other educational games.

Art

Remember the pleasure you received from creating works of art that you proudly took home to mom and dad, like clay paperweights, macaroni necklaces, and colorfully painted dioramas? In art class, first graders will also enjoy the same experiences. What's even more exciting is that art has taken on a much broader scope in today's schools. No longer is art an activity reserved for Friday afternoons. Today, your child will do art across the curriculum. Art projects may stem from your child's work in reading, science, math, or even social studies, making it a more fun and relevant experience.

Content

The arts in the first grade can include anything from coloring and painting to acting or re-creating works from famous artists. Simply put, the goal of arts education in the first grade is to *create*. It's yet another way for your child to express his thoughts, feelings, and ideas about the world around him.

First grade students should be encouraged to express themselves creatively and talk about what they have made. Some specific ideas for art projects include:

➤ Create hanging mobiles
➤ Paint self-portraits
➤ Illustrate the covers of books
➤ Design a class mural

➤ Sponge paint pictures
➤ Use rubber stamps to create personalized greeting cards
➤ Build a piñata out of papier-mâché

Music

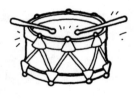

Music education will vary as it competes for time and resources in a school. However, any music program will offer children an important and diverse learning experience. Along with singing songs and playing instruments, your child will learn to appreciate different types of music. Often, children will explore various cultural heritages just by listening to the music of other countries.

Music can also be a great source of pride and esteem for students as they have a chance to shine while creating and performing.

Content

Here is a brief glimpse at what you might find in a first grade music program:

> **Instruments and their families.** Instruments will be divided up into the percussion family, the wind family, and the string family. Some instruments from the percussion family include the drum, xylophone, triangle, maracas, castanets, cymbals, and tambourine. The string family includes the guitar, violin, and banjo. Instruments from the wind family include the flute, recorder, clarinet, and oboe.
> **The orchestra.** First graders are introduced to the idea of an orchestra and a real-life example of instruments and people coming together for a common purpose. This reiterates concepts of family and cooperation.
> **Great composers.** First grade music curricula will usually cover several great composers such as Mozart, Bach, Beethoven, and Tchaikovsky.
> **Favorite songs.** Classic songs will probably be taught such as *America the Beautiful; La Cucaracha; Row, Row, Row Your Boat; Frère Jacques; She'll be Coming Around the Mountain; Take Me Out to the Ballgame;* and *Happy Birthday.*
> Improvise short songs and instrumental pieces using traditional sounds (e.g. voices and instruments) and nontraditional sounds (e.g. hands clapping and fingers snapping)
> Read whole, half, and quarter notes
> Identify by style examples of music from various historical periods and cultures
> Identify various uses of music in their daily experiences

Physical Education

First graders naturally want to move their bodies and exercise. All it takes is a visit to a playground to see children running, jumping rope, swinging from the monkey bars, kicking balls, and chasing one another. Most first graders are active and energetic and sometimes unable to control their energy. As older individuals, we long for a time when we could jump and run and play without a care in the world. At times we find their movements and actions dizzying, but we understand it, and we let them play (safely of course) to their hearts' content before having to tell them that time is up and we must return indoors. It's important to encourage this activity and help lay the foundation for future physical health and well-being.

Content

Physical education in the first grade comes in two forms: recess or actual P.E. (physical education) time. In most schools, first graders have two short recesses and a lunch period. They are timed strategically to make sure that children get to move around every few hours. Children may also have a scheduled time for physical education each week, either with their classroom teacher or a coach. Whatever the case may be, here's what you're likely to find in most first grade physical education programs:

➤ **Skipping, Hopping, and Jumping.** These are basic coordination skills that should be mastered by the end of the first grade.

➤ **Throwing and Catching Balls.** First graders experience an increase and improvement in eye-hand coordination. This makes it an optimal time to teach and practice throwing and catching balls.

➤ **Group Games.** Six- and seven-year-olds show an increased interest in team sports, and it's important that they have opportunities to play them. Some fun group games include kick ball, red rover, and soccer. These games are also a great way to foster cooperation and respect.

➤ **Jump Rope.** First graders have increased control and balance, and jumping rope is a great way to develop these skills even more. In addition, kids love singing the rhyming songs that accompany jumping rope.

➤ **Sports.** First grade marks a real interest for some children to learn baseball, basketball, and soccer. They've probably watched enough pro sports games by this point to recognize famous players and will probably start wearing team jerseys to school.

➤ **Sportsmanship.** Even if your first grader is not the most athletic, there are other valuable lessons to learn on the field. Being a team player and a good sport are more important skills to have than running or catching.

Safety

First graders have a lot to learn about life beyond the classroom. For this reason, many schools offer programs in drug prevention, fire and personal safety, and even earthquake or storm preparedness. Often these are offered as outreach programs in which firefighters or police officers come to the classroom to teach the following:

➤ "Stop, Drop, and Roll"
➤ "Just Say No"
➤ "Never talk to strangers"

If these lessons are not part of your child's curriculum, you are encouraged to teach your child skills to face life outside the class or home.

SUMMARY

The curriculum outlined in this chapter is a sample, but don't worry if your child's classroom differs slightly—all classrooms are unique. Knowing in general what's expected of your child will help you to understand what your child is going through at school when you're not around. With this understanding, you can help him cope with all the new faces, lessons, and rules that accompany the first grade.

3

...And How You Can Help Your Child Learn

▼

So you think teachers have the market cornered on creative ways to encourage your child to learn? Of course, they don't! Below we have compiled a list of the best activities and projects to reinforce what your child is learning in school. Here are a few helpful hints for making the most out of these activities:

➤ Keep the length of activities to about ten to fifteen minutes; activities that are too long or complicated will cause your child to lose interest
➤ Avoid distractions such as TV and video games so that your child can better focus

➤ Make sure your child isn't overtired; any game becomes a challenge when a child is not rested

READING/LANGUAGE ARTS

There are so many wonderful ways to encourage reading at home. Some tried and true methods are listed here. Over time, these practices help reinforce, develop, and build on the basic reading skills your child is learning at school.

➤ **Read together every day, every way.** Read aloud to your child as often as possible. Try to read for at least twenty minutes a day, either reading to your child or having her read to you. Make a routine out of reading such as reading before bedtime or first thing in the morning at breakfast. Even reading the cereal box counts! Besides building on her reading skills, you'll enjoy the quiet time, and your child will cherish the one-on-one time with you.

➤ **Make books a priority.** Help your child learn to value books by modeling how important they are to you. Even if you're not a reader yourself, it's important that your child actually see you reading. We promise that there's something out there that everyone can enjoy. Modeling reading will convey that you value reading and that it's a cool thing to do.

➤ **Buy books as gifts.** Have you visited children's bookstores or the children's section at your local bookstore lately? There are tons of brilliantly illustrated, exciting stories that are sure to capture the attention of even the most reluctant reader. Why not incorporate books into gift giving? Select special hardcovers and write inscriptions in the front. These gifts become family keepsakes to be handed down to the next generation.

➤ **Check out online booksellers.** Online booksellers, such as amazon.com, compile terrific lists of recommendations for all age groups and interests. Often, in addition to a synopsis of the book, readers have posted their reviews. You can take these testimonials into consideration when choosing bedtime stories for your child.

➤ **Go on reading fieldtrips.** Nothing will spark your child's curiosity more than knowing that there are thousands of really exciting books waiting to be read at the local library. Take your child there and let him explore. Make it a weekly event and watch how his enthusiasm grows. Find out if the library has story hours—most do—and go. Get your child his own library card and make a big deal about him having his own card. He'll love the responsibility of being just like a grown-up.

Here are some other creative and fun family activities that can build and strengthen your child's reading skills and show him how much fun it is to learn:

➤ **Produce star-studded family plays.** Have the family retell their favorite aspects of holidays, trips, and stories, and re-create them into plays. Everyone can have a part. It can be as simple as a one-act, one-person play or as complicated as a set-filled and costumed extravaganza. Maybe your kids would prefer to produce and direct puppet theater. Puppets can be made out of simple materials, such as socks, and they will definitely provide hours of entertainment. This is a great way to pass a rainy or snowy day.

➤ **Play with board games.** Scrabble, Boggle, and Wheel of Fortune are just a few games that give kids a fun way to toy around with letters to make words. Add to the fun by playing along and nudging your child to really try to make sensible words. Point out the patterns along the way, and you've got yourself an extra credit, fun-filled activity for the entire family.

➤ **Tell a joke or two.** Encourage your child to learn a few good jokes and work on the timing and tone of the delivery. He'll be thrilled with making people laugh while developing his speaking skills.

WRITING

Lessons in school tend to focus on the technical aspects of writing such as mechanics and punctuation. At home, you can make writing feel more natural and fun for your child. Here are several easy and effective ways to encourage your child to be a writer:

➤ **Be a writer yourself.** The best way to teach your child to do *anything* is to do it yourself. This means keeping a journal, writing letters to family and friends, or keeping shopping lists, all the while making sure your child sees you doing it. Chances are, he'll be curious about what you're doing, and that will give you the perfect opportunity to explain the many purposes of writing.

➤ **Read, read, and read!** Writing and reading go hand in hand. Reading and discussing stories together is a brilliant way to stimulate your child's verbal skills. Asking questions like, "What do you think the kitty will do next?" sparks creativity and planning skills. Your child will learn how to construct a story himself by reading and listening to stories.

Here are some fun ways to encourage your future Shakespeare to develop strong writing skills. You can use this list as a springboard for your own creative ways of building excitement for writing. Have fun with it, and the entire family will benefit.

➤ **Become a cartoonist.** Get out the markers, crayons, construction paper, scissors, and colored pencils to help your child become a cartoonist. Have some examples handy of children's cartoons such as Garfield or Spiderman to show your child how it's done. Guide him along to create his own sequenced cartoon. This is a fabulous way to develop logical thinking skills It also provides a chance for your child to express himself comfortably in writing.

➤ **Real-life writing.** Let your child be a grown-up by letting him do the kind of writing that you do. There are hundreds of ways to help your child become an enthusiastic and skilled writer. The activities listed below will go a long way to spark enthusiasm, offer "real life" practice, and build on your child's writing skills.

•A letter to a friend, relative, or pen pal
•A postcard while on vacation

- Thank you notes or pictures
- Invitations to parties
- A sign for his bedroom door
- Homemade birthday cards

Go on a treasure hunt. Create easy-to-read clues that build upon one another to bring sequencing to life. Your child will be intrigued with the mystery awaiting her and will beg for repeat treasure hunts time and time again. As she becomes a more fluent reader, have her create the clues and hide them.

➤ **Tell stories together.** Children delight in storytelling! When interesting or funny things happen, talk about how this could be turned into a written story. Talk about the beginning, middle, and end of the story. Talk about the biggest problem in the story and how the main character could have solved it a different way.

➤ **Display your child's written work.** Put those stories up in the kitchen, on the front door, or anywhere in the house that is high profile. It will show your child that you value her writing and think it's important. It will also help her begin to feel like a real writer.

MATH

There are so many ways to bring math to life! In the classroom, first grade teachers use manipulatives to make math real for children. Manipulatives such as stacking blocks and jigsaw puzzles are a great way for children to be exposed to hands-on math problems. At home, there are plenty of ways you can make math fun and exciting, too. Here are a few of our favorites that you and your first grader can incorporate into your daily lives. The important thing to remember is that math is—and should be—fun.

➤ **Model math confidence, not math phobia.** The best gift you can offer your child is a strong enthusiasm for math. It is important not to convey feelings of "I don't like math" or "I'm not good at math" because your child may adopt your feelings. Instead, it's better to model that math is important and interesting to you by engaging your child in hands-on math activities that will be sure to spark her enthusiasm for numbers

➤ **Drill basic addition and subtraction facts.** Use flash cards to help your child learn math facts. You can buy them at most toy stores or teacher supply stores, or you can even make your own on index cards. On one side, write the problem such as 3+5, and on the other write the problem and answer 3+5=8. Have your child recite the entire problem and answer each time. Build in a reward system and before long, you'll both be having a great time with math!

➤ **Watch the clock.** Talk about time. For instance, remind your child that it's 7:30—one half hour until bedtime. She'll soon catch on.

➤ **Read about math.** There are many books about math that will excite your child and encourage her to learn concepts such as geometry, measurement, and money. Some good choices include *How Much is a Million?*; *If You Give a Mouse a Cookie*; and *Gator Pie*.

➤ **Build problem-solving skills.** Talk about how to solve real-life math problems. Present a problem such as "How many days do we have to plan your birthday party?" Get out a calendar and ask your child her to count the number of days until her birthday. She can wake up every morning and subtract one from yesterday's number until the big day arrives.

➤ **Encourage careful work.** Help your child learn the value of careful work by encouraging him to go slow, check his work, and consider if his answers make sense. Be sure to praise him along the way, and it won't be long before he's acing first grade math.

There are tons of ways to bring mathematics to life for your child. Below are some of our favorite ways to make math real and exciting for your entire family.

➤ **Show him the money!** Next time you're shopping, let your child try to count out the money to pay. Be sure to give him some guidance, and make sure there's not a line behind you. (The last thing you want are angry customers yelling at you.) There's no better way to teach money than in real-life shopping experiences.

Get cooking.
A great way to teach measurement is by cooking. Let your child measure out the flour for the chocolate chip cookies. Let him pour the milk for the pudding. The more he's actively engaged in the process, the better you can model the importance of measurement.

GREAT IDEA!

➤ **Play math games.** You might be asking—what's a "math game?" A math game is any game that builds on math skills such as counting, using money, strategizing, brainteasers, problem solving, and tests of memory. Some all-time favorites include Monopoly, Uno, Chutes and Ladders, Go Fish, and Old Maid.

➤ **Set up a savings account.** Help your child learn the value of saving money by going to the bank with her and opening a savings account. Help her understand the importance of saving by giving her a certain amount for holidays that goes straight into the account. Be sure you take her with you to deposit the amount, and share the balance with her. She'll be thrilled with the "officialness" of the process!

➤ **Organize "counting projects."** Encourage your child to count how many of certain items are around the house. For instance, one Saturday can be *pillow day*, during which he tallies the number of pillows in the entire house. The next Saturday can be *windows day*, during which he counts all the windows in the house. Keep track of his findings on the computer or in a paper notebook. Your child will be proud of his counting skills when ten or more items in your house have been "officially counted."

> ➤ **Give your child an allowance.** Providing your child with an allowance will help her learn about money. You can also help her develop a sense of responsibility by encouraging her to save it toward the purchase of something she really wants.

SOCIAL STUDIES

There are so many ways you can help bring social studies to life for your child. Here are several ideas that will help personalize and enrich your child's social studies curriculum:

> ➤ **Visit historical places.** There are bound to be historical places around your geographic area, such as parks. The next time your child has a day off from school, go exploring and discover the hidden treasures under your footsteps. This will help bring history to life for your first grader.
> ➤ **Talk about current events.** Make history real by sharing the newspaper, television news programs, and Internet websites with your child. Of course, be careful with the content presented. A little caution and foresight is all it takes to open up the world of current events to your child.
> ➤ **Introduce the concept of discrimination.** You are the best person to model respect and tolerance for others. Help your child understand that discrimination is hurtful and wrong. Share examples of how others have been discriminated against, and discuss ways it could have been avoided. Most importantly, be a model of respect by ensuring that your language, actions, and jokes are free from any biases whether they are racial, cultural, or religious. Make tolerance and respect part of your family life.
> ➤ **Tell your family's story.** Pull up a chair and tell your own family's story including information about grandparents, uncles, aunts, and cousins. Your child will be fascinated with the adventures of his own family. Put together a scrap book or a journey box that holds the photos and stories of your ancestors.

What can you do if you have a budding historian on your hands? Here are some extra-credit activities that will foster enthusiasm and interest in social studies.

Build a family tree.

Work together to trace your family's roots back as far as you can. Today's schools are shying away from this wonderful activity because of the increase in untraditional family units. However, you are in a prime position to teach this in a meaningful and appropriate way for your child. There are even computer programs that will facilitate the creation of your family's lineage.

G R E A T I D E A !

➤ **Record the family's story.** Teach your child the value of different perspectives by having him interview different members of the family. It won't be long before he'll realize that different people have different takes on the same family event. This is an invaluable lesson for any future historian and will build an appreciation for getting all the angles of a story. It's also a fabulous way to get to know the extended family.

➤ **Plan the next family vacation.** Let your future geographer help plan the next family trip. Begin by brainstorming where to go. Then make a "planning chart" of the steps needed to put the trip together. This is also a great way to introduce maps and globes to your child. During the trip, keep a map handy and discuss the route along the way. Also be sure to tell the related historical stories of the area you're visiting. Your child is bound to receive an incredible social studies curriculum just with this experience.

SCIENCE

You have a special role in fostering an interest and enthusiasm for science, especially because of the limited role that science instruction plays in the first grade. Here are some easy ways to get your child curious about the natural world around him. It won't be long before he catches on and begins to build a background in the physical, biological, and chemical sciences.

➤ **Cook together.** The kitchen is a wonderful resource for science, reading, and even math. Find an easy-to-follow recipe and bake something together. The chemical reactions will demonstrate the power of science and will fascinate your child. Point out how liquids turn to solids with heat and how sometimes they will return back to solids if removed from the heat. Your child will think it's magic! Cooking also offers genuine lessons in measurement, reading, planning, and temperature. Its value cannot be overemphasized.

➤ **Read together.** There are phenomenal children's science books that cover the first grade curriculum and beyond. Get reading and before long, your child will be fascinated with science, scientists, and the natural world. Some of our favorite choices include *Germs Make Me Sick!,* by Melvin Berger (Harper Collins, 1985); *The Magic School Bus Inside the Earth,* by Joanna Cole (Scholastic, 1987); and *Amazing Fish* by Mary Ling (Knopf, 1991).

➤ **Act like a scientist.** There is no better way to encourage your child than to talk about scientific events that occur in your home. Don't be afraid to discuss things like the moldy food in the refrigerator, the mildew in the bathroom, the ant problem, and the plants that lean toward the sun. These are all *real* science issues and can be a source of lively dialogue with your child.

➤ **Encourage your child to be a scientist.** It won't take much prompting to get your child interest in collecting and organizing different objects. Ideas for collection include seashells, coins, rocks, and seeds. The process of systematically giving order to objects is a basic skill in science. The best part is that she won't even realize she's doing science; she'll just think she's having fun!

For your budding scientist, here a few hands-on science experiments that cover basic elements of biology, geology, chemistry, and botany. Your child won't know this of course—all she'll know is that she's having a blast!

Tend the Garden

Involve your child in taking care of your house plants. Go over the importance of sunlight, water, and nutrients in the soil. If one of the plants starts to wilt, get your child's input on what he thinks is the cause. Tracking the life cycle of a flowering plant can also be an invaluable lesson in biology.

GREAT IDEA!

➤ **Build an erupting volcano.** Here's a fabulous and easy way to bring science to life. Get a hold of some clay and have your child shape a volcano onto a sturdy piece of wood. Add some twigs and pebbles around the base of the volcano to make it more realistic. Then get out the magic ingredients: baking soda and vinegar. Throw in a couple tablespoons of each into the volcano and voila. It will erupt! Don't worry about a large mess, though. The "lava" will ooze out slowly. Adding red food coloring to the mix can make it even more realistic. Besides being a dynamic activity, this is also a lesson in basic chemistry.

➤ **Experiment with daisies.** Here's a good way to demonstrate how plants absorb water. Set up five different glasses of water. Have your child add about a tablespoon of different colored food coloring to each of the glasses, and then place one white carnation in each of the glasses. Within a day, you'll have multicolored carnations, and your child will have learned that water travels up a plant's stem.

➤ **Make a moon calendar.** Keep track of the phases of the moon with a moon calendar. Let your child use her observation skills to draw the present phase of the moon. Is it full, new, half, or crescent?

COMPUTERS

Here are some tips for how you can incorporate computers into your child's academic growth. In many cases, schools have been slow in taking full advantage of the educational technology available. Tight budgets, training, and facilities are just the beginning of why schools are often in the dark ages when it comes to technology. How can you help? As a concerned parent, there are a number of things you can do. Here's a brief list of the best ways you can aid both your child and his school:

> **Own a home computer.** Having a computer at home is not essential for your child to succeed in school, but it certainly helps. Even if your child does not use it for educational reasons, she will benefit from becoming more comfortable and confident with using a computer. Try to find out what computer system is used at school and, if possible, buy a similar model. This will help your child acquire computer skills even faster and create consistency in her practice.

> **Explore the community for free computer use.** Many local libraries and community centers offer free computer use and often free Internet connections. All it takes is some time and ingenuity and before long, your child will have additional contact time with the computer.

> **Build up your CD-ROM library.** There is an endless array of educational CD-ROMS that are currently available (and many more on the way!) that can greatly enhance your child's learning experiences in the classroom and at home. Spend some time with your child discussing what he likes to do best on the computer. Tailor your purchases along those lines so he'll be sure to like them. Chapter 9 has a list of recommended CD-ROMs for first graders.

ART

Art is all around us in our everyday lives, yet making a special effort to bring art to your child or bring your child to art can serve to pique his interest. Here are some ideas for expanding your budding artist's horizons.

➤ **Explore in the local museum.** Art is also seeing, thinking, and interpreting. By talking about art and exposing children to everyday art as well as special exhibits, students will learn the language of art. By closely examining art and discussing it, your child will begin to develop an appreciation of art that likely would not develop otherwise.

➤ **Read about art and famous artists.** There are beautifully illustrated children's books that will bring the world of art to life for your child. For instance, there are books indicating color, shape, and texture as well as books about the lives of famous artists such as Van Gogh and Picasso. These books can help your child to better understand and appreciate the arts.

Master Class. Enroll in a beginner art class in the community. Check your local Y or Boys and Girls Club for more information about such programs.

GREAT IDEA!

➤ **Art alive!** Let your child experiment with paints, markers, Play-Doh™, glitter, crayons, colored pencils, or anything else with which she can create from her imagination. Display the work from your future Michelangelo to show you care.

MUSIC

Here are some ideas for sparking an appreciation and enthusiasm for music in your child:

➤ **Take your child to see local productions** of musicals, operas, or chamber music at a nearby college or university. You don't have to live in a big city with an esteemed music center to enjoy a good performance.
➤ **Enroll your child in a local music program.** It can be anything from singing to playing the tuba!

G R E A T   I D E A !

Go to your library where your child can check out CDs, and you can foster in her an appreciation for all types of music. Use each trip to focus on a specific genre of music, from classical to jazz, country to rock-n-roll.

➤ **Everything's an instrument.** Show your child how to make music with anything from clapping hands to banging pots and pans. You can even teach her how to whistle!

PHYSICAL EDUCATION

Here are some of our favorite ways that parents can encourage physical fitness and healthy habits in first grade children:

➤ **Be good role models.** Incorporate exercise into your weekly schedule.
➤ **Enroll your child in swimming lessons.** Your local Y or Boys and Girls Club will offer inexpensive lessons. This is also a great way to make friends with kids from different schools!

➤ **Look into martial arts classes in your community.** Karate, Judo, Aikido, etc. not only give kids an opportunity to exercise, but they also establish excellent balance and coordination in six- and seven-year-olds.

SAFETY

Chapter 2 mentioned school programs designed to help your children learn about personal safety. However, these lessons can never be taught too often. Included here are four websites you can visit together to reinforce lessons about personal safety.

➤ **www.usfa.fema.gov/kids/** The United States Fire Administration has created this site specifically for children to teach them about preventing fires and escaping them. Games and graphics make learning about fire safety fun, not scary.

➤ **www.fema.gov/kids/ready.htm** The purpose of this site is to help children to prepare for disasters. FEMA (Federal Emergency Management Agency) uses cartoon characters to teach children many valuable lessons about disaster preparedness.

➤ **www.fda.gov/oc/opacom/kids/default.htm** The Food and Drug Administration has created a site complete with games and quizzes to teach children about everything from food safety to preventing tobacco usage.

➤ **www.cpsc.gov/kids/kidsafety/main1.html** Even the Consumer Product Safety Commission has a site to teach children how to reduce the risk of injury related to consumer products. Kidd, a friendly goat, leads children through games about safety.

There are so many other things you can do at home to ensure your child understands the importance of safety. Here are a few basic ideas to get you started.

Teach your child his name, phone number, and address to ensure he knows how to contact home if lost.

GREAT IDEA!

➤ **Create a family password.** By establishing a password, it is less likely your child will go home or wander off with someone who doesn't know the magic word.

➤ **Fire Safety.** Teach your children not to play with matches and what to do if a fire occurs. Have an escape route planned out, just in case. Try to make it fun, not scary for your child.

➤ **Have an alternate emergency contact.** If anything ever happens, chances are that you, as a parent, will be contacted first. However, if the occasion arises that you can't be reached, have another family member or close family friend as someone your child can call if she needs help.

➤ **Post emergency numbers by the phone.** Make sure your child understands the importance of 911 in real emergency situations. The number for the police, the fire station, and the local hospital should be posted at every phone and someplace accessible such as the refrigerator.

Although your child's teacher will have a set agenda taught in school, as a parent you can introduce effective and creative ways to support her learning outside of the classroom. When your child sees your interest in her subjects (and their applications to the real world), she'll be more inspired to study what's going on. As one of your child's principle role models, your behavior toward academics will make a difference in her attitude and efforts. Don't be alarmed if your child doesn't glide through all of her subjects with ease. The abundance and content of material presented in first grade can be very challenging. But as a parent, you can be excited—not to mention fascinated—by the way your child's hard work and efforts eventually fall into place as she begins to figure things out. Watching your child's face light up as she suddenly understands a concept is an irreplaceable experience. And the confidence you instill in her by taking time to support her learning will give her a wonderful start to grade school.

4

Your Child's Social Development

▼

There's a lot more to know about your first grader's school experience than just the ABCs. On the whole, first graders typically have a wonderful natural ability to laugh. Jokes and riddles can keep them entertained for long stretches of time. Your child will also be eager to display her new accomplishments at home and at school. She will show a marked enthusiasm for games and new play ideas. Accompanied by these enjoyable qualities, your child will begin to acquire new life skills such as negotiation, respect, confidence, and cooperation—traits that will help her interact well with others. These skills will be intrinsic to your child's well being as she segues from half-day or all-day kindergarten to first grade.

What are the social skills associated with first grade? First graders are expected to learn how to be independent while mastering the fine art of **getting along with others**. Most of the social skills associated with six- and seven-year-olds revolve around this common theme. These skills include **cooperation, self-control, respect for others and self,** and **responsibility for one's actions.** While some of these skills are introduced or learned at home, first graders will develop many of them by interacting with their new friends and teachers at school.

THE IMPORTANCE OF SOCIAL SKILLS IN THE FIRST GRADE

First grade represents a giant leap into a new and exciting social network for children. For some children, it's the first time they've been in a full-day, structured school setting with people other than their family and friends. Other children—the seasoned full-timers—also have some new social demands awaiting them in their first grade classroom. There will be a more structured schedule, a variety of academic subjects, the cafeteria, and perhaps even thirty or more children in the room. Needless to say, it's going to be a challenge for both the novices and the pros!

To be successful, first graders have to figure out how to make friends, take turns, compromise, work together and alone, and manage some self-control. Chances are, your child will feel more confident academically and emotionally when these skills are mastered. The teacher will play an important role in fostering these positive traits in your child, and many of the lessons she teaches will include a sidebar or two on getting along with others.

You may begin to wonder how your child's doing in the realm of "social skills." Experts have many different opinions regarding which skills are necessary *before* entering first grade and which are necessary *after* completing the first grade. Of course, every child is unique and will develop at his own pace. For example, some will have mastered self-control but still be shaky with responsibility. This is okay. What's important is that you have a sense of the standard—what's generally expected of first graders by the end of the first grade. The following checklist is a broad overview of common traits the average six-year-old has before entering first grade:

➤ Wants to be the center of attention
➤ Has seemingly limitless energy
➤ Has difficulty being flexible with decisions or actions
➤ Is attached to adults including parents, caregivers, and even siblings
➤ Is often on the verge of tears
➤ Needs to be the "best" or "winner" at games and activities
➤ Is silly, demanding, critical, and often unreasonable in expectations

The following is a checklist of social goals achieved by the end of the first grade year:

➤ Works independently for *at least* twenty minutes
➤ Is flexible with decisions and actions
➤ Begins to learn from his or her mistakes
➤ Communicates feelings, needs, and opinions
➤ Is self-controlled
➤ Is able to keep hands to self
➤ Thinks before speaking
➤ Respects self and others
➤ Participates well in groups

THE TARGET SOCIAL SKILLS
OF FIRST GRADE

Now that you know where your child should be at the end of the first grade, it's time to take a step back and figure out how to help him get there. There are six target social skills for first grade children. These social skills lay the foundation that helps children adjust to first grade life, make lots of friends, and be successful in school now and in the future.

➤ **Cooperation.** A child's success and happiness in life will depend upon her ability to get along with others. She must learn to take turns, play fair, and cooperate with others.

➤ **Assertion.** It's important that first graders learn to express themselves clearly and be able to communicate their feelings to others. This will help them succeed in the classroom and on the playground.

➤ **Self-control.** First graders will also be expected to work and complete assignments on their own. Sometimes this will involve quietly working at their desks for twenty minutes or more. It's important that they keep their hands to themselves and not distract those around them.

➤ **Responsibility.** First graders are expected to know how to listen to directions and be able to follow them. Sometimes this means multiple-step directions that can pose difficulty for even the most adjusted child. Being responsible in a first grade classroom means knowing what needs to be done and *doing* it.

➤ **Respect.** First graders must learn how to respect everyone and everything around them. This involves thinking before speaking, keeping their hands to themselves, and treating others with care and courtesy. Many teachers refer to this as "The Golden Rule." A teacher in Hermosa Beach, CA, reminds her class on a daily basis to "Remember the Golden Rule: Treat others as you would like them to treat you." This makes a lot of sense to six- and seven-year-olds.

➤ **Empathy.** First graders must learn how to relate to the feelings and needs of others. This involves sharing and knowing how it feels to "be in the other person's shoes."

The methods that teachers use to foster these social skills vary from classroom to classroom. However, most first grade teachers make room for the development of social skills by setting up classroom rules, modeling good behavior, and using role-playing to help students learn to deal with conflict. Other teachers simply allow students to interact naturally and handle differences that they encounter on their own. When trouble arises, students are encouraged to go to the teacher for help in solving the problem.

To get a better perspective of the social world of first graders, we've interviewed several different teachers. We asked them how they go about helping their students learn the social skills listed above. Here's what they had to say:

Blanca Perez, a bilingual educational evaluator from New York City, says *assertion* is one of the biggest social problems she's seen in first graders. "Kids either assert themselves too much, to the point of aggression, or they're passive." She does role-playing activities that help students deal with conflict progressively. "In a role-playing activity, I might present a conflict to the students and have them come up with solutions. If a child comes up with the answer 'tell the teacher,' I prompt her to come up with more effective ways to solve the problem on her own."

Lisa Carron, a reading specialist from Norfolk, Virginia, says *self-control* is one of the biggest social problems she's seen in the classroom. To help her students learn to control their words and actions, she uses lots of positive reinforcement. "If my students are lining up and everyone is wiggling and talking except a few well-behaved students, I take time to praise the self-controlled children in front of the rest of the class: 'Look how nicely Maria is lining up!' I also use a sticker system, where I give a sticker for every good behavior I observe. At the end of the month, I give out prizes to students with a certain number of stickers."

Ms. Carron also says there should be heavy emphasis on developing *responsibility* in the first grade classroom. "Fostering responsibility in children at this age promotes organization. If a child is expected to complete homework on time and complete class projects on his own, he's going to develop the necessary organizational skills along the way." She also says that parents and teachers shouldn't be afraid to let children take responsibility for their own mistakes. "Parents shouldn't bring in forgotten homework—if a child makes that mistake once and suffers the consequences, she's less likely to make it again."

Leslie Jackowski, a first grade teacher from Pennsylvania, says that *respect* is one of the most important skills for her students to master. "A major goal of my first grade classroom is for students to learn to respect everyone and everything. One way I help students learn respect is through a game we play. Each morning I gather my students together and one student spins the spinner on a board with various good deeds listed. The spinner could land on *address an adult correctly, pick up trash, say please and thank you,* and a variety of others. Whatever the spinner lands on, that's the courtesy my students will practice that day."

Another social skill Ms. Jackowski makes time for in her classroom is *empathy*. "In first grade, kids are starting to realize it isn't an ideal world. They don't *always* want to share, and they don't like everyone in the class equally. Kids then have to learn to reconcile the differences in what they've learned is right and what they're feeling. One way we work on this is to play a game I've found called "You Hurt My Feelings." It consists of a variety of cards with different feeling-hurting scenarios. I read aloud the scenario, which could be something like, 'You painted a picture for your good friend. When you gave it to her, she tossed it on her desk and ran off to talk to someone else. How did that make you feel?' Then a discussion ensues, and the students and I talk about how the friend could have behaved differently and why it's so hurtful to feel unappreciated."

Marcy Lublin Ed. M., CAGS, an elementary school psychologist, made these observations about first graders:

"Social skills are directly correlated to how one gets along with others. Important skills at this age include listening, sharing, following directions, and self-control. First graders are beginning to become more selective in their peer relationships."

THE 10 MOST COMMON SOCIAL PROBLEMS

Typically, first graders have some difficulty making the adjustment to first grade. Although school settings vary, we've found that children across the country display similar behaviors. Here is a list of the ten most common social problems in the first grade:

1. **Testing the waters.** First graders will test the limits of rules and see how much they can get away with. Consistency and fairness helps keep them in check and tame the intrigue of seeing how to bend the rules and get what they want.
2. **Over-reliance on TLC (tender loving care).** First graders are known for needing lots of Band-Aids and comfort, especially in the first few months of school. They are also known for frequent stomachaches and will worry and fuss about other ailments.

A parent in New York relates this story of her first grader:

We went through a period of time when my son was complaining of stomachaches and not feeling well. It turned out that this was all because he didn't want to go to school. I couldn't imagine why a child so young was having anxiety about school, and I was sure that it wasn't because he did not have friends since he has always been outgoing. I talked with him about it, and eventually he expressed that he really hated having to read out loud and to do creative writing. At the time, these were his problem areas. We were able to get him some tutoring for his reading, and this was a great experience for him. As he became a better reader, he felt more confident and the stomachaches disappeared."

3. **Cheating in games.** Like all children, first graders like to win. They'll often be sneaky to come out ahead, even if it means having to lie to cover their tracks.
4. **Tall-tales and other fantasies.** First graders love a good story and often embellish the truth to make stories more interesting. As fun as this sounds, the teller of tall tales may find some of his peers disputing the facts. First graders are also intrigued with fantasy and enjoy playing dress-up and other make-believe games. This activity is healthy as long as the child does not withdraw, preferring to spend time alone in a fantasy world.
5. **Quantity over quality.** At six- to seven-years-old, children are into speed. They want to hurry through work instead of taking their time and doing a good job. Their race to finish and do more often makes their work sloppy. This may translate into a social problem because children will also rush to finish games, activities, and

assignments in which other children are involved. This can lead to anger, frustration, and impatience that will very often lead directly into disagreements with others.

6. **Feelings of incompetence.** First graders like to create projects and want to do a job well. As the famous cognitive scientist Erik Erikson coined it, six- to eight-year-olds are in the "Stage of Industry." All this means is that this age group needs lots of opportunities to apply the skills they are developing. They need to feel sure enough of themselves to take risks and struggle with challenges to reach a goal, solve a problem, or complete a task.

7. **Good guy vs. bad guy games.** First graders love power games in which two opposing sides are at battle with one another. This explains their fascination with Power Rangers, cowboys and Indians, and cops and robbers. If left unchecked, these types of experiences can promote hostility between children and prompt them to be mean to one another.

8. **Talkative, sassy, and just plain noisy kids.** First graders are usually excited to be in school and want to share every thought that comes their way. They can be chatty, loud, and disruptive as they go about doing this. Six- and seven-year-olds often need direction to become respectful and responsible in class and at home.

9. **Bullies.** Believe it or not, bullying happens even in the first grade. Children need to learn to not be easily intimidated by bullies and to assert themselves in a positive and constructive way. Most importantly, they need to respect themselves and others and be tolerant of differences. This can help them to avoid conflicts and become more socially skilled.

10. **Don't want to share.** Sharing is one of the hardest skills for first graders to learn. We're not just talking about sharing material objects, either. First graders are learning the importance of sharing time and space as well. Whether it's learning to wait one's turn rather than blurting out the answer or sharing friends rather than excluding others, first graders are learning that they are part of a whole rather than the center of the universe.

The fact that your child may display some of these behaviors is not necessarily a sign that she is a "problem child." Remember these are typical traits, but as a parent, you can help guide your child into more responsible and healthy interactions with others around him.

WHAT YOU CAN DO TO HELP

Parents play an important role in helping develop and refine their children's friendship-making skills. As you know, you are the best source of support and encouragement for your child.

Here are some sure-fire ways of helping your child acquire the all-important social skills to help her excel in first grade both academically and socially.

> ➤ **Set good examples.** Your child is watching you all the time. Parents' reactions to their spouses, other children, and friends provide children with models of appropriate (or inappropriate) behavior. Remember this and make a commitment to do everything you can to set a good example of social skill behavior for your child.
>
> ➤ **Watch your child's interactions with others.** It's important to pay attention to your child's interactions with others. Does she share? Is she overly bossy and telling others what to do? Is she afraid to speak up in a group? These observations will help you determine if your child is doing okay socially or if some intervention may be in order. If interventions are needed, the sooner you take action, the better.
>
> ➤ **Get to know your child's playmates.** It's a good idea to know your child's friends well so you plan fun activities that will not only hold their interest but also minimize conflict. If you know they both like swimming, chances are they'll be motivated to cooperate and get along. On the other hand, if one child dislikes a scheduled activity, there's a high likelihood of a fight erupting.

Help your child develop communication skills. Parents play an essential role in building children's communication skills. You will model either effective or ineffective communication skills. Here are some tips to improve your communication with your child so she can, in turn, develop strong communication skills.

- Be interested and attentive to conversations
- Ask questions about her day

GREAT IDEA!

- Ask how he's getting along with her classmates
- Listen patiently
- Share your thoughts
- Let your child have his say without interrupting or finishing thoughts for him.
- Pay attention to body language such as posture, facial expressions, and attitude.

➤ **Arrange play-dates.** Encourage opportunities for your child to interact with others. Invite children over to play or arrange for a "date" at the park. Various opportunities to play together in an unstructured setting will give your child a chance to test the waters and experiment with new social skills without the constraints of school rules and schedules. A child is far more likely to test his social skills at the park than at home with a box full of Legos.

➤ **Emphasize cooperation and compromise.** It's critically important to emphasize, remind, and reinforce cooperation and compromise. Six- and seven-year-olds often want to do things their way rather than compromise. You can help change this by making suggestions about alternative ways of solving problems. For instance, if your child seems unable to solve a conflict, intervene with concrete suggestions about how to solve the problem. Say something like, "Try X and see if it works. If not, come back and we'll try and think of something else."

➤ **Help your child to cope with disappointment.** Again, one of the best ways to convey this life skill is by modeling it yourself. When you're dealing with a disappointment, let your child in on it. This way, he knows that disappointment is a fact of life, not something personally designed to bring him down. For example, maybe you didn't get that promotion that you were up for at work. Admitting that you are disappointed, but showing that you're able to accept the situation at work—leave for the office in a cheerful mood, and mean it when you say that you're happy for your colleague who got the position—is setting a good example for handling life's disappointments for your child.

➤ **Help your child develop a new skill or hobby.** Perhaps the simplest suggestion of all is to help your child acquire a new skill or interest that will allow him to fit in with his peers. Some suggestions include sports, dance classes, arts and crafts, and musical instruments. This new interest will provide new concepts for your child to talk about, while also helping her feel more confident and self-assured. Most likely, she'll even make a few new friends along the way.

Teacher's advice

All of the teachers with whom we spoke emphasized the vital role that parents can play in shaping their child's social habits. Samantha Youle, a teacher in New York reminds parents that bad behavior is an opportunity that they should take to problem-solve with their child. "A child who misbehaves is acting out for one reason or another. Talk to your child about why he's acting the way he is. Just spending time together and talking is the best way to get through difficulties. And don't be afraid to discuss things that *you've* done wrong in the past."

Leslie Jackowski encourages parents to respect their child's decision-making responsibility in the home. "Parents should have children come up with the rules. When they've written the law, they're much more likely to understand and follow it." She also says that instead of just saying "no" to a child's request, parents should take the time to discuss why something is denied. "If you don't want your child to go outside and play before her homework is done, don't simply say 'you're not going outside.' Hear her out; ask her to provide reasons why she should play before homework. That way, she has a chance to articulate her own ideas, and you'll be showing respect by taking the time to listen."

Blanca Perez also advocates teaching respect by modeling it.

"Parents need to focus on orienting their children, rather than commanding them to do things. For instance, if your child's room is a mess, rather that ordering to clean her room, talk her through the reasons why the room has to be clean. Say something like, 'You know that clothes belong in their drawers, or they'll get in your way and become wrinkled,' rather than simply saying 'I said get in there and clean up that room!' This approach will help your child understand that his responsibilities have a purpose and that you're not just trying to make him miserable." Ms. Perez also offers the advice that parents and educators need to be aware of the tone of their voices and make sure the way they are speaking is the way they would want to be spoken to.

Other things with which your child may have difficulty with include:

➤ Keeping friends
➤ Entering or joining a group
➤ Dealing with teasing
➤ Considering other people's feelings
➤ Losing her temper
➤ Being unable to make simple decisions on his own
➤ Overreacting to failure or disappointment

A parent in Seattle offered this advice in helping his son who is prone to crying and getting frustrated easily:

"My son is a sensitive soul and tends to cry easily and often. Remember, each child is an individual. Sometimes, when I feel that the event he is crying over is trivial, I will remind myself that he is more sensitive than I am and tailor my reaction to fit him. I will *listen* to him and try to see his point of view, but I will also try to show him why the situation is not as big of a deal as he believes. Then, we work together on a solution."

Try not to be alarmed if your child has difficulty with some of these areas. It's common and even *expected* that there will be some issues with adjusting to the first grade. Sometimes a good heart-to-heart talk is all it takes to start the social-skills ball rolling in the right direction. Don't be afraid to ask your child, "Hey, how are things going at school?" Children are amazingly frank and honest if asked the right question by someone they trust. Listen to your child and pay attention to her problems. Discuss different ways she could have handled a sticky situation. Ask her how the other person may have felt. Role-play and practice better reactions. What's important is that you develop a trusting, open relationship with your child. This will show her how to express her feelings while validating the feelings she's having. Over time, she'll open up and give you a clearer picture of what's going on in the classroom and elsewhere. Talking with her may be the most effective way to combat minor glitches in the development of strong social skills.

FACING MORE SERIOUS SOCIAL PROBLEMS

Okay, so you still fear that your child has a problem with social skills. She loses her temper frequently and can't seem to make friends. You've tried the suggestions above and they don't seem to help. The important thing to do at this point is to identify and acknowledge the problem so you can take the appropriate action to help your child overcome her difficulties. The good news is that social skills can be learned and first grade is the perfect place to start.

Whatever problem your child is facing, with your support, patience, and willingness to work with the teacher, you can overcome it together. Here are four fundamental steps you can take to helping your child overcome a social problem:

1. **Talk with your child.** As a first step, find a quiet place to talk about your concerns with your child. Ask some general questions that will help spark discussions like, "I see that sometimes you lose your temper. Why do you think this happens?" As sensitively as possible, describe to him what you have observed or heard and help him discuss how he feels about it. Be sure to focus on specific behaviors such as anger or frustration so he can relate to what you're talking about.

2. **Talk to your child's teacher.** It's important to talk in a confidential and discreet manner with your child's teacher to see what's happening at school. This will help you understand how your child relates to others. Ask questions such as: What are her strengths? What are her weaknesses? Do the social difficulties happen in isolated incidents associated with a particular situation? Or, are they ongoing problems that have become repeated patterns that make her unpopular and sad? If your answers fall into the second category, you'll need to take some action.

3. **Try to pinpoint the problem.** Keep trying to identify the source of your child's difficulties. Talk with other parents, family, and friends who spend time with your child. Get their honest opinions about what's going on. Answer the questions in the section above and then ask "Do you think my child has a problem with social skills?" to get a better sense of where the problems may lie. Your goal is to try and find the aspects of social

interactions that create the most problems for your child. For instance, does she have trouble reaching out to others in a friendly way? Does she have difficulty keeping a game or conversation going? Does she solve problems with physical or verbal violence? By doing this, you'll get a better sense of where the problems may be so you can better help your child.

4. **Seek professional help.** Sometimes serious problems are causing or contributing to your child's difficulty with social skills. These might include stress within the family, medical problems, emotional difficulties (i.e. anxiety, acute shyness, or anger), speech and language problems, or attention deficits. Needless to say, there are numerous factors that could be influencing your child's inability to develop social skills. If you suspect that problems such as these are making things worse, seek out advice from your pediatrician or another professional.

A NOTE ABOUT SELF-ESTEEM

Children need healthy, earned self-esteem. What is earned self-esteem? The concept has been variously defined but certainly includes:

➤ A sense of who you are—an appreciation of your own individuality
➤ A judgment of yourself as a basically good person
➤ A judgment of yourself as a capable person
➤ A recognition that you are capable of successfully interacting with other people

How can you tell if your child does not have these essential good feelings about himself? First, don't rush to judgment. Bear in mind that children, like grownups, have their movements of uncertainty, days when they are convinced that no one likes them and that they cannot succeed at anything. So occasional bouts with low self-esteem are to be expected—let it ride. The problem is serious when these behaviors go on and on and dominate the child's outlook.

Here are some worrisome indications of significant low self-esteem:

The child constantly makes negative remarks about his or her abilities:

➤ "I'm too stupid to do this problem"
➤ "I'm not good at anything"
➤ "I always get the wrong answer"

The child refrains from normal social exchanges:

➤ She is convinced that no one likes her
➤ She refuses to have play-dates
➤ She won't try new activities such as trying out for soccer
➤ She is afraid to participate in class; for example, she won't raise her hand to answer a question

The child is easily upset:

➤ When his work is corrected
➤ When a friend mildly insults him
➤ When a sibling outperforms him

Beyond Self-Esteem Issues

Low self-esteem can sometimes be a signal of something more serious—clinical depression. In cases of depression, the manifestations of low self-esteem are more emphatic and sustained. Additional symptoms of depression include unrelenting sadness, too little or too much sleep, dramatic mood swings, and a refusal to play with other children. Don't ignore these indications. If you suspect that your child might be suffering from depression, do something about it immediately. Have your child see a professional therapist as soon as possible. It is terrible to spend years of one's childhood feeling despondent and it is your responsibility as a parent to do what you can to help.

How to Improve Your Child's Self-Esteem

So what can you do to help enhance your child's self-esteem? A great deal.

Recognize that, for better or worse, what you do is crucial. Self-esteem is about having positive feelings about yourself and, for a young child, those feelings depend most importantly on believing that one's parents share that positive assessment. Children of first grade age need to know that the adults who matter in their lives care about them, like them, and approve of them. When that assurance is not there, a child's self-esteem is severely undermined.

Joshua Halberstam, Ph.D., offers this list of ways to help your children feel good about themselves:

1. Promote self-esteem, not narcissism or self-absorption.

Try to get your child to focus on experiences and activities, not just her vague feelings. For example, when your child returns from a trip to the circus, instead of asking her general questions such as, "Did you like it?" ask for specifics such as, "What did you like best about the circus?" Or "What act surprised you the most?" The point is to get your child to focus on the experience, not just her own responses.

2. Use praise as a genuine response, not as a tool.

Feeling good about achievement spurs children to achieve more. Kids recognize when they are being bluffed. If adults always tell them that they have done well, children conclude that either adults have low expectations of them or that adults have poor judgment. Either way, praise soon loses its value. Praise only when you mean it.

And, praise is much more appreciated when it is directed to particular outcomes than generalities. So instead of always responding to your daughter's drawings by saying "Sherry, you're a magnificent artist," give her specific feedback such as, "Sherry, that's a wonderful letter 'G' you wrote," or "Those are great ears you drew on that monkey."

3. Listen, *really* listen to your child.

Active listening is a crucial element in nourishing self-esteem. Remember to take your first-grader seriously. Respect your child for the developing intelligent person he is. Pay genuine attention to his complaints and needs as well as his joys. When your child tells you of his worries, "We all go through that," shouldn't be the end of the conversation, but the beginning. Get to the heart of the matter together, and implement an action. When you and others treat your child with respect, he is much more likely to develop self-esteem.

4. Have reasonable expectations for your child.

Your children need to know that you have high but reasonable expectations of them; that way, they can develop high but reasonable standards for themselves. Telling your child that you think he is old enough to put his dirty clothes in the hamper or that you expect him to do his homework each day demonstrates your belief in his growing maturity. Giving children responsibilities makes them feel useful and valued.

5. Allow your child to have his or her own personality.

Some personality styles are routinely mistaken for poor self-esteem. Shyness, for example, is commonly confused with a lack of self-esteem. But a kid who's shy in most social settings can be, for example, aggressive and confident on the soccer field. Introverted behavior is not necessarily a sign of low self-esteem either. Nor, for that matter, is extroverted behavior always a mask of underlying low self-esteem.

6. Turn failures into learning experiences.

Self-esteem is critical to coping with failures, so it's important that you help your child develop this skill. This means, first and foremost, not pretending that your child's unhappy experience wasn't painful. The next step is teaching your child coping skills. You might remind him, for example, of past failures that turned out not to be so bad after all. You know your child best and will recognize which strategies are most effective in his particular case.

7. Be a role model for self-esteem.

As with everything else, parents are the central role models for children, especially for children at this vulnerable age. So let your children know that you feel good about yourself. Show them that you also make mistakes and have learned from them. This, of course, is easier said than done. To pull this off, you really do have to like yourself and learn from your mistakes.

Be available.

Your child needs to know that what she does matters to you. Talk to your children about their activities and interests. Go to their games, show up to parent-teacher meetings, and attend their plays and award ceremonies. Your involvement demonstrates to your child that what is important to him is important to you. Your involvement shows that you really care about his life. This involvement goes a long way in reinforcing a young child's self-esteem.

THE SOCIAL TRANSFORMATION OF YOUR CHILD

The excitement of entering grade school and discovering new things and friends will attract your child to the classroom, but some kids will adjust more quickly than others to the new sets of rules, responsibilities, and challenges. Your child will be in an environment where he will have to exercise a new sense of self-control and respect for others. You as a parent can help by being a role model, communicating with your child, and encouraging positive social interactions. The social transformation of your child from kindergarten to first grade may at times feel rocky, but by consistently working with your child in the ways mentioned in this chapter, you can help establish positive behavior patterns that will prove invaluable in the future. In return, you will have the pleasure of discovering your child's ability to learn new behaviors, participate academically, make new friends, and become a more mature being.

5

The First Grade Partnership:
Your Child, Your Child's Teacher, and You

WHERE YOU WILL FIND:

➤ What to expect from your child's teacher
➤ What to expect from your child
➤ What to expect from yourself
➤ How to establish strong communication
➤ Ways to help your child focus on schoolwork at home

Wouldn't it be great to be a fly on the wall in your child's classroom and watch as he moves through his day in school? You could see academic areas where he excels, areas that need more support, the outgoing or shy qualities that overtake him in the company of his classmates, and many other fascinating elements that make him a unique individual. Unfortunately, unless you yourself are a first grade teacher, you won't be witness to these kinds of things. But the happenings between drop-off and pick-up time don't have to be a mystery to you. On the flip side, your child's time between the end of the school day and the beginning doesn't have to be a mystery to the teacher.

By maintaining a direct line of communication between your child's teacher, your child, and yourself, you will develop a stronger understanding of your child's overall personality and academic performance. In a partnership, the three of you can work together to help your child build the right study skills, learning habits, and behavior that are so important to a successful first grade year.

How do you begin to build this partnership? A good place to start is with a frank discussion of *expectations*—from your child, your child's teacher, and, most importantly, from yourself. Each of you plays an important role in your child's first grade experience. Your child will need to work hard academically, act responsibly, and learn how to be independent. These new expectations may seem intimidating at first to a six- or seven-year-old, but with hard work and effort, she will begin to settle in and enjoy her new life in grade school.

Your child's teacher also faces some challenges. She will try to be fair with all students and adjust the classroom pace to meet the needs of each student. Some straight talk about reasonable expectations and how to work together to create the best learning situation possible for your child is what this chapter is all about.

Last but certainly not least, there is *you*—the caring first grade parent. Because you know your child the best, you will be the supportive foundation upon which your child relies. You will learn how to use this knowledge of your child in a way that encourages—not discourages—development and growth.

With an understanding of the expectations of these three elements (your child's teacher, your child, and you), you can begin the communicative partnership that will support your child from the beginning to the end of first grade.

WHAT TO EXPECT FROM YOUR CHILD'S FIRST GRADE TEACHER

First grade teachers have one of the toughest jobs in the schooling business. They're responsible for teaching your child to read, write, add, and subtract while helping her become an independent learner and listener. All of this is supposed to happen within the six or so hours of the regular school day. Sound impossible? Well, it can be without strong teaching skills and a whole lot of help from school staff and adult volunteers.

Within the bustling school environment, parents often wonder if their children's educational needs are being met. What's fair to expect from your child's first grade teacher? Based on our years of teaching experience and teacher interviews, we've come up with what we think is a fair and reasonable list of expectations for your child's teacher. Use this knowledge to better support what's going on in the classroom and possibly initiate constructive conversations with the teacher.

Lisa Majeski, a teacher in New Orleans, LA, uses a color-coded chart to illustrate the behavior of her students.

Each time a child is warned, he or she "changes her color." Once a child gets to black, she goes directly to the principal's office. While this doesn't happen often, Ms. Majeski attests to the effectiveness of consequences. Her students know what to expect if they misbehave. This helps keep them on the right track and focused on learning.

➤ **Respect for All Children and Cultures.** Your child's teacher will respect all children, treating them with the dignity they deserve. This also means providing appropriate education for each child. Discrimination of any kind is not only morally wrong but also against the law.

➤ **Classroom Rules and a Behavior Management System.** First grade classrooms will have a prominently posted set of *classroom rules*. Most center on the idea of *respect* but may also include keeping hands to oneself, raising hands to speak, and listening to the teacher. Along with the rules, it's also expected that there is a system to keep track of how these rules are followed.

➤ **Communication with Parents.** It's fair to expect communication from and with teachers. It's the most effective way of keeping track of your child's progress. Most teachers we spoke with were happy to communicate more regularly with parents either through notes, phone calls, or conferences. The common theme, however, was that the *parent initiated the communication.*

Classroom Constitution

▼

1. Always raise your hand.

2. Walk, don't run.

3. Line up before leaving the room.

4. Put toys and materials away.

5. Speak one at a time.

6. Respect others and their things.

Brenda Staples, a first/second grade teacher in Downey, CA, gives a weekly homework packet and finds that most students are able to complete the work by Friday. The time during the week allows them to ask her for help if they need it as well as helping their parents juggle schedules to find quality time to work on homework. A schedule such as this one helps children and families plan ahead and decide how to attack the different assignments.

➤ **A Consistent Homework Schedule.** Your child's teacher will establish a consistent homework routine that's fair and meaningful. Most first grade teachers assign homework on a weekly basis; that is, a "homework packet" is given on Mondays to be completed and turned in by the following Friday. If your first grader does not seem to have a homework schedule, it's a good idea to talk to her teacher. Perhaps there is a schedule that your child hasn't understood, or maybe the teacher has his reasons for not establishing a consistent schedule. The best way to find out is to mention your concerns to the teacher and work together to better understand the homework process.

➤ **Reasonable Homework Assignments.** Most first graders receive ten to fifteen minutes of homework a night. The United States Department of Education believes that homework is most effective for children in grades first through third when it does not exceed twenty minutes each school day. Talk with your child's teacher if you are concerned about either too much or too little homework.

➤ **Interesting and Worthwhile Assignments.** Simply giving homework assignments is not enough to foster real learning. Assignments have to be worthwhile and interesting for students—especially first graders—to value them. Children learn little from busywork—dull, repetitive exercises that may lead to boredom more than learning. This is especially true in math. Completing page after page of the same type of addition problem teaches little to the competent student. The less able student, who needs review the most, may get frustrated and spend time practicing mistakes. Homework is effective when it's at the appropriate level of difficulty.

➤ **Constructive Comments.** Homework can help children learn if they understand that it's an important part of the learning process. This happens when teachers take the time to provide children with feedback about their work. Sometimes all it takes is a "great work" stamp on the top of an assignment to give children the positive feedback needed to validate their hard work and effort. Even better is when teachers write comments that reflect the quality of the work. Like adults, children need honest and regular feedback about their work. It helps them to understand specifically where they made their mistakes and how they can fix them. It also helps them feel confident with their strengths, giving them the incentive to work on their not-so-strong skills.

Mitchi Dragonette, a teacher in Hermosa Beach, CA, emphasizes the importance of honest feedback on homework. She will write comments such as "Good work but try to be more careful with your printing." She finds that children often turn work back in with the corrections made.

WHAT TO EXPECT FROM YOUR CHILD

Your child has a starring role to play in the first grade. As the student, she will be responsible for learning how to read as well as progressing in the other first grade learning standards. However, her responsibilities go far beyond just learning the minimum competencies. Your child will need to be a partner—together with her teacher and you—in the learning and homework process. She needs to develop the all-important study skills and learning habits that will help her be a successful student in the later grades. This means buckling down and being serious about her work. It also means gradually becoming more independent with her reading, school assignments, and homework.

It's often tough to figure out what exactly to expect from a first grade child. Here is a no-nonsense list of what most first grade parents can expect from their children. While no child is the same, this list of expectations will help you know how much to help and where to draw the line. Most importantly, it gives you a clear sense of the all-important role your child has in the learning process. The bottom line is that nothing can happen without her participation. It's up to you to help her realize this early on in the first grade.

➤ **Respect for Self and Others.** First graders must learn how to respect everyone and everything around them. This involves thinking before speaking, keeping their hands to themselves, and treating others with care and courtesy. It's a fair and reasonable expectation that your child treat others and himself with the most respect possible. If he treats others this way, it won't be long before he has made new and lasting friends in the first grade.

➤ **Genuine Effort.** It's important that your child try her hardest to understand, complete, and turn in her assignments. This effort is tantamount to the entire first grade program. On the flip side, if your child does not exert the necessary effort, it will undermine any efforts by the teacher or yourself. No matter how hard the two of you try, you cannot do the work for her. Well, you can, but it won't help in the long run. It's important to set the stage now by modeling the benefits of strong, genuine effort. Your child should be expected to always give 100 percent effort no matter what the subject, assignment, or project. As we all know, good effort often translates into better grades and a deeper understanding of the material.

➤ **Hard Work.** Like genuine effort, hard work is another important ingredient in the recipe for a successful first grade year. There is no doubt that your child will have to work hard to make the transition to first grade and learn how to read at grade level and master basic addition and subtraction facts. She'll also have to work hard at becoming independent and completing assignments on her own. Learning the value of hard work early on will help steer her in the right direction.

➤ **Responsibility.** One of the hardest things for children to learn is how to be responsible. They often forget papers, avoid picking up after themselves, and lose things. However, being responsible is a necessary factor in being a good student. It is expected that first graders act responsibly in the classroom and at home. They must take care of not only their own supplies but also those of the class and their families. Most first grade teachers will assign homework with one goal in mind—to build responsibility. First graders have to understand what the assignment is, gather the necessary papers and supplies, carry the work home, and talk about the assignment to you. Without a doubt, this is a lot to ask of a six- or seven-

year-old. However, with your patient and consistent support, it won't be long before your child becomes a responsible learner.

➤ **Positive Attitude.** At some point during the first grade
year, you may encounter a reluctant child that becomes
cranky at the thought of going to school or doing homework. First find out if there is any validity to the cranki-
ness: Is someone at school bothering him? Is the work too
difficult or too easy? Does your child want or need extra
attention in general? As a parent, it's reasonable to expect
a positive attitude from your child. You can support this
attitude by acting as your child's role model and express-
ing your own interest in the subjects studied. Because
your child is constantly taking cues from you, your own
interest will incite hers. You can also stick to a consistent
study schedule. The more consistent you are with her, the
more consistent her attitude toward doing work will be.

WHAT TO EXPECT FROM YOURSELF

Last but not least, there is *you*—the hard-working, dedicated parent who is doing everything possible to make the first grade year
a positive and successful one for his child. The good news is that
you're already well on your way to exceeding every expectation
for parents nationwide. You've made a sincere effort to educate
yourself about becoming an involved and caring first grade parent. Now, we'll offer some food-for-thought about new and perhaps different ways of supporting your first grade child and her
teacher. We've listed various ways to become involved inside the
classroom and out. All of them are tried and true methods that
have worked for parents over the years.

➤ **Be your child's role model.** First and foremost, be your
child's role model. It is through your actions, rather than
through "talking," that your children will come to understand exactly what you value. As such, if you have a plan
in place to handle homework, your child will know how
important this work is. As your child's role model, you
will also show him how to become an organized and diligent worker. As you work on your own projects in the
evening, share with your child the steps and the strategies
you use to complete your work.

➤ **Get to know your child's teacher.** The sooner you get to know your child's teacher, the better. Establish rapport early on and let the teacher know that you're a caring and supportive parent. Once you have started a relationship, it will be easier to discuss progress and review any special needs your child might have.

➤ **Get involved in your child's classroom.** If you have the time, observing your child's classroom is a good way to know what's going on with your child at school. Schedule a visit during a particular class, a half day, or whole day. Your child's first grade teacher will be able to accommodate you if she knows in advance. You can also offer to help out with specific projects or chaperone a field trip.

➤ **Be a reading role model.** There are many ways you can help your child become a reader. For starters, you can read with him, tell him funny family stories, have books and other reading materials in the house, take him to the library, and discuss the daily news. There are thousands of other ways to encourage your child to become an avid reader. The goal is to provide all of the support you can to help your child see that reading is fun and exciting. This is the best gift you can give him for his future success in school. If he acquires and develops strong reading skills now, chances are he'll excel in later grades.

➤ **Equip your child with the necessary gear.** Your first grader should be well equipped with necessary materials for the classroom and for doing homework. For first graders, these materials will likely include: crayons, pencils, markers, erasers, glue, construction paper, rulers, writing paper, stapler, scissors, etc. Having these materials also available in one specified area at home will cut down on familiar homework excuses such as "I don't have any paper!" which children may use to divert their attention elsewhere. Here's a starter list of supplies and resources for your first grade child:

- Pencils
- Pens
- Erasers
- Pencil sharpener
- Writing paper
- Construction paper
- Glue or paste

- Tape
- Paper clips
- Crayons
- Markers
- Stapler
- Hole punch
- Children's dictionary

➤ **Praise and support your child's efforts.** Remember that you must encourage and support your child. If he has been doing a good job with his school- or homework, he should be told so.

➤ **Set up a study schedule.** As a parent, it's your responsibility to choose a daily Homework Hour for your child and to stick with it. It's up to you to model responsibility, commitment, and follow-through with "homework time." This time should be chosen keeping in mind that a responsible adult should be available to assist your child in any way necessary. Your child may want to put off homework and make excuses until bedtime. The solution is to schedule homework into your child's daily routine. Be sure to consistently review your child's daily homework schedule with him. This will ensure that your child understands your expectations for homework.

➤ **Designate a proper study area.** Your child must have a quiet place in which to work. His study space should be free of the distractions caused by television, music, or younger siblings. It's a good idea for you and your child to choose the location together. This location should be close enough so that you or another responsible adult is easily available for help.

➤ **Establish yourself as an involved parent.** While homework will be the focus of the following chapter, it is critical that you understand that your child must be held responsible for completing her own homework each night. You must make clear to your child that while you know at times the work will be difficult, she is expected to do it. Stop in from time to time to offer her support and encouragement. And, after she has completed her homework, review it for quality and accuracy.

When your child does not understand a homework assignment, follow these steps:

➤ Ask your child to read the directions

➤ Have him explain it to you in his own words

➤ If he can't do this, break the directions down into parts

➤ Ask questions concerning how the assignment is to be done until it "clicks"

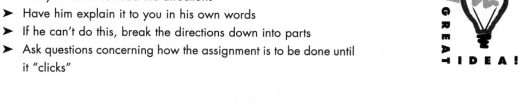

G
R
E
A
T
I D E A !

➤ **Establish consequences for your child if she does not abide by the homework rules.** If you have created rules concerning homework in your home and your child has yet to abide by them, there must be consequences for this type of behavior. Determine for yourself what these consequences will be and, more importantly, be sure that you enforce them.

A Final Note on Homework

The primary goal of first grade homework is to build study skills for the upcoming years. These skills include learning to follow directions, working independently, beginning and completing tasks, and managing time. Homework will also help teach your child responsibility. It is up to her to bring it home, do the work, and make sure that it gets back to school. These are difficult skills to tackle at the ages of six to seven. That's why homework can be a great way for parents to get involved in the process and help their child become a successful student. Studies show that homework, when done conscientiously, has a positive effect on academic achievement. And as children move up through the grades, homework becomes increasingly important to school success.

While first grade homework may only take up to twenty minutes per night, it is still important to take it seriously and encourage solid effort. It is a mistake to think, "She's only in the first grade" or "She won't have much homework anyway." First graders *will* have homework, and they will be expected to complete it in a thorough and timely manner. Whether your child gets five or forty-five minutes of homework a night, it's up to you to see to it that it gets done. In fact, it's *expected* that you'll help your child figure out the assignments and complete them.

As the parent, you're in a prime position to get involved and be your child's homework helper. This is the year to begin to develop homework habits that will be needed as your child makes her way from first grade through college. It is not too early to begin thinking about homework skills. Rather, if you wait, it will be much more difficult to establish a solid studying pattern for your child.

Communication

Like a thread, communication will bind your child's teacher, your child, and you together so that you can solidly form a team to support your child's first grade experience.

At home, organizing and working on homework together is itself a form of communication. You can observe your child's approach to the work and see if he struggles with a particular problem, and you are there when your child has a specific question. You can also casually ask specific questions that let you know more about his school life. If you're not sure where to begin, here are a few suggestions:

> ➤ What books are you reading in school?
> ➤ Do you raise your hand in class?
> ➤ Who do you like to sit next to?
> ➤ What is your favorite subject? Why?
> ➤ What did you do in science class today?

Simple questions like these will encourage your child to think more about what's going on around him while giving you some information about what he may be like at school.

The first grade teacher, however, is not as accessible as the child you bring home every night. The following is a list of opportunities you can utilize to build and maintain a good communicating relationship with your child's teacher throughout the school year. the more both of you know about your child, the more both of you will understand how to enrich his first grade experience.

> ➤ **Open house.** First grade teachers use an annual Back-to-School Night or an Open House to display the material kids will be learning in first grade. It is held after work when parents can visit the classroom. It's up to the first grade teacher to decide how the Open House is conducted. An open house is a fun and exciting event where the parents can end up sitting in pint-size classroom chairs facing the teacher. A teacher may give a slide show, display homework samples, and/or give a mini-lecture on the topics studied. If something is

unclear about the material, don't hesitate to ask specific questions, however it's important to approach your child's teacher in a non-confrontational light. Don't forget she has worked hard to organize the Open House and probably isn't used to speaking to a room full of adults.

➤ **Parent-Teacher Conferences.** These are one-on-one conferences lasting between twenty and thirty minutes with just you and the teacher. There are two scheduled during the school year: one at the beginning of the year, and one toward the end. Parent-teacher conferences are an excellent opportunity for you to find out more specifics about your child. The teacher will probably have a set routine she goes through. She may begin with showing you some of your child's work samples, artwork, the books your child is reading, and other things. But you as a parent will benefit even more if you come prepared. Because the teacher will be talking with dozens of parents on the same day, she might not hone in on specifics that you want to cover. Before going into the conference, brainstorm on any glitches your child might have encountered with homework or ask your child if there is something about reading or writing that he likes or dislikes. You can bring any useful information you gather into the conference so that the teacher can be aware of it in her classroom. Once you inform the teacher of things she might not already know, you can then elicit information from *her* about your child. Some sample questions include:

➤ Does my child seem to be concentrating in school, or is he distracted and restless?
➤ In what subjects do you think he has strengths and weaknesses? How can I help in the weaker areas?
➤ Personalitywise, what do you think are his strengths and weaknesses?
➤ Is my child making friends? Who are they?

Maureen Murray, a teacher from Nyack, NY, says this about Parent-Teacher communication:

To ensure a child is progressing to her fullest potential, there must be strong communication between parent and teacher. I encourage parents to volunteer in the classroom and stop in when they're picking their child up from school. Impromptu conversations help keep both of us informed about what's going on in the child's life.

➤ **Initiated conferences.** It's good to discuss any topics of concern with your child's teacher whether it's about someone in class bullying your child, specific academic problems, or special circumstances in the home such as divorce, death, or illness in the family. You may be tempted to pull your child's teacher aside for a mini-conference as you drop off or pick up your child from school, but this is not recommended. First grade teachers are incredibly busy, and their minds are accounted for every minute of the day. If there is something specific you'd like to discuss with the teacher, schedule an appointment or a phone call—even if it's just for five minutes. If your child's teacher knows you want to discuss something ahead of time, when you meet or call, she will be much less distracted and can internalize the information more effectively. There may also be occasions when the teacher calls you into a conference to discuss your child. If a teacher calls you in for a conference, it's natural to feel concern, but don't lose your head. Remember that this is a meeting to accelerate your child's well-being. Find out what the topic of discussion will be. Is it your child's behavior, academic performance, or something else? If you think about the topic before discussing it, you will find the actual meeting to be more productive, and if both parents are involved in the child's life, both should attend the conference. This will shed more light on the subject at hand.

THE THREE-WAY PARTNERSHIP

When you drop off your child at school in the morning, it's easy to detect the anticipation she feels at beginning a new day. She may feel a little excited at the prospect of learning something new, not to mention the idea of being around other fun-loving, good-humored first graders. You can help maintain this feeling of excitement by being an active part of her experience, along with her teacher and herself. As the school year progresses, the importance of this partnership will become more and more apparent. But don't wait until mid-year to get it started. Begin right away with knowing what to expect from your child's teacher, your child, and yourself. From here, you can begin a continuing dialogue with each member of the partnership to ensure your child's first grade experience is the fullest and most fun it can be. Once your child sees that his teacher and you are collectively interested in her progress at school, he will be more likely to take an active role in his own well-being.

6

The First Grade Problem Solver

▼

WHERE YOU WILL FIND:

➤ How to help your child get organized
➤ How to prevent your child from procrastinating
➤ How to help your child focus
➤ How to assess your child's after-school homework program
➤ How to help without actually doing the homework

What if your child won't pay attention in class? What if he won't stop playing video games long enough to shrug his shoulders when you ask him about homework? Many parents have these and other common concerns as their first graders make the adjustment from kindergarten to an all-day school routine. This chapter will present typical first grade problems and discuss real-life solutions.

It's likely that you'll recognize and identify with some of the profiled first grade hassles that follow. Reading through the questions and answers here will help you to identify the issues in your home. You'll be able to adapt the advice to your own first grade child and maybe even to her brothers and sisters later on.

A common problem in the first grade is adjusting to nightly homework assignments. For this reason, many of the problems presented in this chapter relate to homework hassles encountered in the first grade. Most commonly, parents wonder about how to get their child to do her work by herself. It's important for parents and children to learn coping strategies now so that homework becomes just another task that has to get done before the day is over instead of a nightly battle that will wage on for years to come.

Answers to important questions such as how much you should help your first grader with his homework and when to set limits will be covered. You will find out how to know if you're helping or actually *doing* the homework for him. It's a tough—but vitally important—distinction to make. You'll know when to lend a hand and when to stay behind the scenes so that your child can develop the all-important study skills necessary in first grade and beyond.

When you're finished reading this section, it's likely that you'll feel a sense of relief because you'll know that other parents experience the same type of school-related issues as you. Your goal is to help your child become the independent, successful student that you know she can be, and we'll help you to achieve it.

FIRST GRADE QUESTIONS & ANSWERS

How can I help my son remember to bring his homework home?

The simple solution to this hassle is to help your child get organized. A *backpack* or *bag* for books will make it easier to carry homework to and from school. Be sure to take your child along with you when you buy the bag. If she picks out something she likes, she'll be more likely to take good care of it and *bring it home every night*.

A second idea is to purchase a homework folder. Many teachers use this technique to get children organized. Students can safely tuck their assignments into the folder and carry it home with them. An added benefit is that you'll always know where to find the homework, and before long the homework will be making it home on a regular basis. If the teacher does not supply a homework folder, it can be purchased inexpensively at a local store.

Another idea is to talk to the teacher. She'll probably have some unique insights for your child to help her remember her homework. Maybe a note taped to your child's desk saying "homework" is all it would take to remind your child to pack up her work and get it home. Solid communication with the teacher is always a good idea when immersed in a homework hassle.

My child has trouble tackling the weekly spelling list, and no matter how hard we try, she never seems to know the words by Friday. Are there strategies that can help?

Helping your child learn her spelling words can be a fairly easy process; the secret is working on the words *every day* in *different ways*. In other words, practice, practice, then practice some more. Flash cards are a fun and useful way to learn the words, but not the only way. Here are some other ideas.

G R E A T   I D E A !

Have your child trace the words in shaving cream. Take a cookie sheet, spray some foaming shaving cream on it, and help your child sound and trace each letter. Once the word is spelled correctly, practice breaking it apart and re-writing different sounds. Your child will be enjoying the mess so much, she won't even realize that it's "work."

Draw a picture in the center of a piece of paper and write the words in a circle around the picture. Encourage your child to draw a picture that shows the meaning of one or more of the words. Then, when the picture's done, your child can write the words around it. As he is writing each word, it's important that he sounds out the letters and reads the complete word. It often takes three or more times to make it around the picture. This is a great way to reinforce and drill the spelling words.

By using these examples and working with your child during Homework Hour, there is no doubt that she'll become a star speller!

My child procrastinates and ends up staying up late every night to finish the work. How can I help?

This is one of the most common homework hassles. Children, especially first graders, will use every trick in the book to avoid doing their homework. Some famous excuses include being hungry, thirsty, or tired. Meanwhile, you're pulling out your hair as time ticks by and the work still isn't done.

How can you solve this homework hassle? By scheduling a nightly **Homework Hour**. As discussed in Chapter 5, Homework Hour should be scheduled just like other activities in your child's life. During this "hour," your child must read, practice printing, draw, or work on homework. He cannot spend the time playing Gameboy, coloring, or doing anything else unrelated to school. As a parent, it's your responsibility to choose a daily Homework Hour for your child and to stick with it. It's up to you to model responsibility, commitment, and follow-through with the scheduled time. It won't be long before your child picks up on the seriousness of homework and gains the benefit of getting homework done and out of the way so that he can enjoy nighttime with family sharing activities such as reading, playing board games, or watching a favorite TV sitcom together.

I have a slow-working child. It takes her much longer to finish assignments than most of the other children in the classroom. At home she rarely finishes her homework. Should I be concerned?

There isn't an easy answer to solving this first grade problem. Each child is unique and has his own internal programming that regulates how he approaches and completes work. Some children naturally work fast, while others are slower and more careful. This is all okay if the work is being completed in a timely fashion. However, what do you do if your slow-working child takes all day or night to finish the work? The trick is to uncover the factors that slow down the work for your child and quickly troubleshoot the problem so he can finish the homework (and still have time to be a child). Here are some questions you should ask yourself and some solutions to address the problem:

➤ *Is your child disorganized?* If your child's papers and books are a mess, then she probably doesn't know where or how to begin the homework. Help her get organized by buying a backpack or book bag to transport her work home. A folder to hold the work will also do the job. When she can easily find the homework, it's easier for her to actually do it.

➤ *Is there a lot of noise and commotion in the house?* It's important to think about *where* your child is doing his homework. Is it at the kitchen table while you're cooking dinner and talking on the phone? Does she do her work in the family room with the television on and her siblings playing around her? If so, then your child may be distracted by the commotion around her. This will slow her down and possibly triple the time it takes her to finish her work. The easiest way to solve this homework hassle is to set aside a special place that is quiet and away from the distractions of the telephone, television, radio, and family. This can be in a bedroom, a study, or even in the backyard if it's quiet and there is a table upon which to work.

This will help your child concentrate and finish the work in a timely way.

➤ *Is your child a poor time manager?* Maybe your child tries to do too many assignments at once. It's important to help him plan out his Homework Hour. Together, you can talk about what he should do first, second, third, and so on. Your child should do the hardest work first when she is most alert and fresh. The easier things should be left for the end when she has less energy and concentration. Also stress the importance of completing one assignment at a time. This will help your child understand the work and build momentum to get it done.

➤ *Is your child having trouble in school?* Sometimes children learn at different speeds within the same grade level. Developmentally, some first graders pick up reading quickly while others don't get the hang of it until the end of the first grade. Perhaps your child is progressing a bit slower than the rest of the class. Homework may be the first glimpse you get of a possible problem at school. Pay close attention to the work to find out what's going on. It won't be long before you see specific areas that need to be worked on. This will enable you to do some extra work with your child to help her practice the skills with which she's having difficulty. It will help her work faster and get the work done. However, if she's still having difficulty over time, then you should talk with the teacher to find out what is happening and concrete ways to intervene.

The teacher has just told me that my child doesn't pay attention in class. He daydreams or bothers the kids around him instead of doing his work. How can I help when I'm not physically in the classroom?

There may be multiple factors at work that combine to make your child not pay attention in class and not get his schoolwork done. The first step is to uncover the reason why your child refuses to do his schoolwork. Find out what your child is feeling so you know how to attack the problem. Begin by having a frank discussion with your child about school. Ask questions such as, "How do you like the first grade?" or "What is your favorite thing to do in school?" Encourage him to be open and honest. You may discover that he's having trouble with certain subjects and cannot do the homework by himself. Or, the work may be too easy for him and he is bored. Talk to his teacher about some extracurricular activities that may keep him occupied and engaged in his studies.

A second step is to talk with your child's teacher. The teacher has first-hand knowledge of your child's progress. Share your thoughts with him and problem-solve together to get your child on the right path. If your child has confided that the work is too easy, perhaps the teacher will allow him to read quietly at his desk once he's finished. Or maybe your child needs some extra help to get moving. Sometimes all it takes is some extra explaining of directions for kids to feel confident about tackling the work. Perhaps your child just needs a quick "check-in" with the teacher during the work time.

Trace Gordon, a teacher in Downey, CA makes sure he checks in with those children who have "attention" problems. He simply walks by their desks and asks how things are going. The extra attention does wonders for those children who are chronic day-dreamers. It literally keeps them on track.

An added benefit of communicating the needs of your child is that the teacher will know you are actively involved in your child's schooling. Together you can figure out the proper incentives, study techniques, additional resources, and appropriate ways to help. This is bound to increase the communication and cooperation between school and your home and get your child focused on getting his work done.

If you have spoken to both your child and your child's teacher about the possibility of a more serious problem than simply not paying attention, then it might be time to consult with your family pediatrician for an evaluation.

When I try to help my child with his homework, I often find myself doing a lot of it for him. He is now relying more and more on my help. Am I setting a bad example for him?

Many frustrated parents find themselves doing more and more of their children's homework. In reality, this is not helping the child at all. By doing the work for them, parents send a strong message to children that they are not capable of doing the work on their own. Over time, this can chip away at a child's motivation and enthusiasm for school. Without a doubt, the best help you can give your child is to encourage him to do the homework on his own. Be sure to read the last section in this chapter entitled "Determining

How Much Help is Enough" for some specific tips on how to gauge the appropriate amount of homework help for your child.

Something to consider is the possibility that your child may suffer from an attention deficit disorder (ADD). Talk to your child's teacher if you feel that your child is exhibiting signs of ADD. There are certain telltale signs of a possible problem. The early warning signs include:

- Difficulty organizing work and gives the impression he hasn't heard the directions
- Easily distracted
- Impulsively acts out
- Difficulty following directions

My child is spending too much time on homework. How can I tell if there is too much?

First of all, investigate the reason. Is your child "goofing off" between math problems? If so, getting her to focus by sitting down with her will save a lot of time. If your child is able to focus but is still working on homework until late at night, ask her teacher what is the maximum amount of time the assignments should take. If your child works way past the time limit, discuss this with the teacher, and together you can pinpoint the problem. It may be that your child is repeating errors, struggling to read certain words, or that the teacher didn't realize the extent of the work.

See the sample weekly assignments your child is asked to complete. Knowing what is expected of you will help you judge if a teacher is assigning too much homework.

Sample Homework Assignments

▼

Monday:	Write numbers one through ten
Tuesday:	Math worksheet and five minutes of reading
Wednesday:	Practice writing spelling words
Thursday:	Math worksheet
Friday:	Read ten minutes over the weekend

My first grader gets so nervous she can't do her homework.
How can I help her calm down?

Homework is meant to be a positive experience, especially in the first grade. It should encourage children to learn by allowing them time outside of class to explore subjects in new and different ways. If homework causes your child undue stress and anxiety, it's important to think about the way homework is dealt with in your home. Is Homework Hour a battle every night? Do you have to threaten your child to get her started? If so, it's not surprising that she gets so nervous she can't do the work.

Homework should never be used as a punishment. Instead, use positive reinforcement to encourage your child to have confidence with her work. Some effective strategies include using praise for work well done, incentives such as shared reading with mom or a treat before bed, or actual homework help from a willing adult or older sibling. Sometimes children just need a little nudge or assurance that they are not in it all alone. These suggestions will help your child slowly become more independent and confident with her ability to do her own homework.

My child is stubborn and won't do homework on his own.
When I don't sit with him, I end up getting complaints from
the teacher that his work is incomplete. How can I help?

A reason for giving first graders homework is to help them develop good learning habits. It can teach children to work independently and encourage self-discipline and responsibility. As a matter of fact, homework often provides first graders with their first chance to manage time and meet deadlines. Some thrive on the challenge and others flounder. As the parent, you should expect to provide a reasonable amount of support and guidance to help your child learn how to tackle homework.

If your child absolutely will not do the work on her own, then some additional interventions are necessary. The first suggestion is to talk to your child. Find out what her attitude is toward homework and why she won't do it alone. Is she nervous about doing a good job? Is it too difficult? Is she disorganized with papers, books, and supplies? Is it too easy? Does she understand what the assignment is? This information will help answer the question of why she won't work alone and help you formulate an action plan to get her working independently and successfully.

The next suggestion is to find out how your child learns best. In educational circles, this is often referred to as a *learning style*. Simply put, a learning style is the way a person learns best. Each child is different and therefore learns in different ways. Your goal is to find out how your child learns best and then base homework on your child's individual learning style. For instance, some children learn when they come into physical contact with the material. They need to handle, poke, or prod it. They are tactile learners. Many children are visual learners while others learn best if they *hear* the information. And then there are those who do best when they combine various learning styles. If you understand something about the style of learning that best suits your child, it will be easier for you to help him do his homework.

Here are some helpful hints for the various learning styles:

> *Visual Learners.* Does your child learn things best when she can *see* them? If so, drawing a picture or a simple chart may help her with some assignments. For example, if the homework is to write a few sentences about a book she has read, it may help to draw a picture first. You can fold a paper into three parts and label each part *beginning*, *middle*, and *end*. She can then draw a picture for each part of the story. This will help her organize her thoughts and give her visual clues to help her write sentences.

> *Auditory Learners.* Does your child learn best when he can *hear* things? Too much written material or too many pictures may frustrate him. He may need to listen to a story or have directions read to him.

> *Tactile, Hands-On Learners.* Does your child understand things best when she can **touch** or **handle** them? She may need manipulatives, such as blocks or bear counters to help her solve math problems. Puppets and dolls also can help bring reading assignments to life for tactile learners.

My first grader plays computer games on his PlayStation or Gameboy all afternoon. How can I tear him away without a fight to get him to do his homework?

Why not try to incorporate his love for computers with his Homework Hour? Homework can help children learn to use resources such as libraries, reference materials, and encyclopedias. There are fabulous CD-ROMS available that house this type of material (See Chapter 8 for some suggestions). Or why not use computer time as an incentive to get the work done?

The important thing is to emphasize that homework is the priority and must be done before other *fun* stuff. This will help your child learn responsibility, commitment, and time management, some of the most important skills fostered by completing daily homework assignments.

A parent in Huntington Beach, CA has a rule that Homework Hour is done right when her first grader gets home. However, once he successfully completes the hour, he can play electronic games all afternoon until dinnertime. Needless to say, the child likes the arrangement, and the parent is relieved that the homework remains the priority and is done while her child is still energetic and alert.

My child doesn't understand her homework, and for the life of me, I don't understand it either. How can we solve this problem?

It is a problem if both you and your child do not understand the assignments. Don't worry. It's not a factor related to your child's (or your own) level of education or intelligence. Often, first grade homework is directly linked to the lesson presented in the classroom. If you weren't in the classroom that day, then chances are you won't be able to figure out the lesson. A good example of this is a math counting lesson using teddy bear counters to organize numbers into sets of tens. This makes perfect sense if you have the teddy bear counters in front of you and have participated in the lesson that instructs you how to group the bears. However, first grade teachers often assign homework based on the same concept taught in class. Unless you're a teacher yourself, your child won't have the bears with him at home, and you won't know what's expected of your child. Furthermore, if your child didn't understand the work in the classroom, he cannot explain the concept to you so that you can help him.

If this situation sounds familiar, or if other assignments have stumped you and your child, the best thing to do is work together and brainstorm possible ways of figuring them out. If twenty minutes or so has passed by and you haven't made any progress, write a note to the teacher explaining your attempts to do the work. This note should be friendly and descriptive of your combined efforts. Be prepared to receive an explanation the following day and then to be responsible for finishing the incomplete work. In the meantime, the Homework Hour should be filled with other learning activities such as shared reading, printing practice, and math problems. This way, your child is still getting involved in the routine of nightly homework even though it's not the assignment given. Of course, if the assignments continue to be confusing, it's probably a good idea to schedule a parent-teacher conference to talk about the situation more in depth. The teacher will appreciate knowing how much you and your family values learning.

What should I think if every day my son says that he doesn't have any homework? Is this normal?

It's a pretty safe bet that most first graders across the country have homework each night of the week. What will usually differ from school to school is the *amount* of homework given, not whether it's given at all. If your child insists that there is no homework, you will need to do some investigative searching to find out the truth. The first place to look is in his backpack or book bag. You may find a stray paper stamped "homework" or a packet with instructions for parents. Then, it's a matter of motivating him to do the work. If you don't find a thing, the next step is to talk to other parents while you're waiting to pick your child up from school. It won't take long to find out if there is homework. However, the foolproof way of learning the homework policy is to talk to the teacher. She will be able to answer the question of whether there is homework, and if so, what the expectations, time frames, and goals of the program are. Once you learn what the homework policy is, then you are ready to become a homework-helping parent.

Most teachers want to encourage your child to organize her assignments. Often they will provide children with an assignment sheet so that the child learns the responsibility of keeping track of assignments and so that parents can know what is expected of the child.

Homework Assignment Sheet

▼

DATE ASSIGNED	DATE DUE	ASSIGNMENT	PARENT SIGNATURE	COMMENTS

How do I keep my "worker-bee" daughter busy? She finishes her homework in record speed and wants more.

Wow—what a lucky parent you are! It's important to foster this love of learning with some enriching activities, so your child remains enthusiastic and interested in school. There are some wonderful suggestions in Chapter 3 to supplement the regular school day included in the section *How Parents Can Help*. Some favorites include visits to libraries and children's bookstores to acquire new books, computer learning games, and educational fieldtrips. A word of caution—go easy on your hardworking child. Praise her efforts, but don't put unnecessary pressure on her to keep up the accelerated pace. Learning goes through phases, and she may slow down and decide she wants to play outside instead of doing homework. We all can't keep up a frantic pace all the time. As long as she's doing what's expected, you can have peace of mind knowing she's right on track.

As a working parent, there's so little time to be together. The last thing we want to do is fight over homework. How can we find time together after the homework is done and before bedtime?

Try turning Homework Hour into family hour. Homework doesn't have to be drudgery—it's all in the attitude. Homework can bring parents, children, and educators closer together, creating a "team" approach to the schooling of children. It also helps parents stay abreast about what's happening in the classroom and provides ways they can build on this learning at home.

Schedule homework time as an actual daily appointment, an hour dedicated to homework, reading, sharing stories, or other similar activities. During this time, TV, computer games, coloring, and playing are not allowed. TVs and radios are turned off. Some families even use it as a family homework time. Everyone does something to help his or her own learning. Mom and/or Dad can be reading the newspaper or a novel while other siblings are doing homework or reading.

You'll be amazed at how comforting this time can really be. Before long, you'll be looking forward to the quiet family times in which you can relish your learning as well as your whole family's experience. Most importantly, the screaming and fighting over homework will silently disappear because your child will want to be a part of the action.

The after-school program offers homework help, and it seems to be working. How can I be sure?

Communication is the best way to monitor your child's homework time in after-school care. Talk to the coordinator of the program to discuss her expectations of your child and to find out the specifics of the homework help available. Is it one-on-one help with a low ratio of students to teachers? Or is it a larger group setting with a few adults to supervise?

Because your first grader will need one-on-one help, your child should opt out of the homework time if there is limited help and enjoy other resources of her after-school program. You can work together when you get home. Also, if the after-school homework help is less than fifteen minutes, you'll need to supplement extra homework time at home.

It's also a good idea to talk directly to the person or people that work in the homework help program. Discuss their expectations of the children and how they feel about helping them with their work. Use your "parent radar skills" to get a feel for the situation. If you feel that the person is right on target with his expectations, then chances are your child will benefit from the help.

Regardless of who provides homework help to your child, *you* should continue to monitor her work to make sure it's being done responsibly. For example, on the way home from the after-school program, ask her questions about her work. Find out how it went, what was hard, what was easy, and what she still may need to work on. That way, there will be clear communication between your child and you and it will help you stay actively involved in the learning process. In other words, just because the work is already done before you get home, it doesn't mean you are off the hook with your responsibility to share in your child's learning.

The good news is that many after-school programs do offer quality homework help that's supervised by at least one certified teacher. It can be an incredible resource to have your child complete the homework while in after-school care so that when your family comes together at the end of the day, you can do family things such as having dinner together, reading books, and playing games. Your role can be to better prepare your child to bring the resources, books, and supplies necessary to make the best use of his homework time at his after-school program.

Use television as an educational reward

There are many terrific educational programs available, as well as videos that can be rented, that will reinforce learning and enrich the curriculum. For example, if your first grader is studying the ocean in science class, there are fascinating programs and videos available that will bring the ocean to life. The bottom line is that television does not have to be a distracting, unpleasant part of the homework process. Use it to your advantage, and it won't be long before your child reaps the benefits as well.

My daughter insists on doing homework in front of the TV. Is this bad?

Yes, doing homework in front of the television is a dangerous habit to fall into in the first grade. While the work may be easy enough to do with limited concentration, it won't be long before it gets harder and more demanding. Don't encourage a bad habit now that will have to be undone in the years to follow when homework gets more serious and time-consuming. If you think it's tough to get her away from the TV now, just imagine how it will be with a couple of years of habit under her belt. It will be impossible to tear her away. Instead, it's better to use television as an incentive to get the homework out of the way and completed by a reasonable time.

My first grader is so exhausted by the time we get home from school that there's no energy left for homework. What are we doing wrong?

Without a doubt, today's first graders are a busy bunch. After a full day of school, many first graders begin a non-stop series of "appointments." Some head off to dance class and sports, while others attend music lessons and play-dates in the after-school hours. It's not surprising that children might collapse into bed after such a full day. However, it's important to treat homework with the same commitment and timeliness as these extracurricular activities. Homework's an important part of the schooling process and must be a daily part of a first grader's life. How do you fit it in? Only you can determine the best daily time for homework in your home.

The first thing to consider is how busy your child is. If homework cannot fit into the current line-up of events, perhaps it's a good idea to re-evaluate the schedule and cut out some activities. Remember that first graders need some unscheduled "me time" to develop independence and creative thinking skills. Also, think about what time your child goes to bed and what he's eating. Sometimes first graders need more sleep than they are getting to support their grow-ing bodies and minds. The same goes for their eating habits. A healthy diet goes a long way to support an active schedule.

DETERMINING HOW MUCH HELP IS ENOUGH

Now that you know how many glitches can come up in the homework process, how do you know how much to help? It's tough to know when to draw the line in the sand and pull back from helping your first grader with her work. You want to be a star parent, and so far you've made a career—or second career—of taking care of your child.

However, it's important to remember that sometimes the best way to help is not to help *at all*. Yes, sometimes in life your child will have to brave through things on his own. Working through problems on his own will help your child develop the critical thinking skills that will help him wade through life in a successful way. First grade may seem awfully young to begin the process, but it's never too early to help your child develop the wherewithal to face difficult tasks, strategize, and implement an effective plan to work through them.

Your role is to *facilitate* the homework process, not to be an active participant. You should be looking over your child's home-work, but don't do the work. He may need some help getting focused and started. It's perfectly fine to help him get organized and to plan out which assignments he'll tackle first. However, your child should attempt to do the work *on his own* before ask-ing for your assistance. Remember, homework is ultimately *his* responsibility, not yours.

What's the best way to help? Encourage your child to do her best work and to try her hardest. You'll be there when she needs clarification about directions and support to keep trying and not to give up. You can make sure she has a quiet place, supplies, and resources to complete the homework. Most importantly, the best way to help is to make sure your child knows that you're in it together—that you'll be by her side every step of the way to guide, support, and encourage her to be the best student she can be. Before long, she'll grow to be more independent with her work and more willing to try before asking you for help. In other words, she'll be well on her way to becoming a grown-up second, third, and even twelfth grader. The time to begin the homework process is now, so get motivated!

7

Challenging Your Child

▼

So, you've got an especially curious and bright child. She seems to understand things quickly, problem-solves with ease, and constantly questions how things work and why they happen. It's exciting to sit back and watch how your child can process the information around her, but don't think your work is automatically done. Sometimes having a bright child can be as big of a challenge as having one who struggles in school.

Children who "get things" quickly often demand a lot of attention and can be easily bored with school and activities. Just ask any first grade teacher. Sometimes the most restless children in the classroom are the top readers or star mathematicians. Once they've sped through their work, they look for new, more stimulating diversions. This can result in talking out of turn, answering questions before other students have had a chance to think, temper tantrums, and a lot of unnecessary noise that ends up interfering with the progress of other students.

It's important to find ways to challenge your child—to keep her curiosity alive and kicking. This way, she'll look forward to school, give it her best effort, and see the value of learning. If she doesn't see the value of school, it won't be long before she becomes reluctant in the morning when its time to leave or refuses to do her homework. There's no better time than the first grade to get the wheels in motion to keep your child interested in learning.

In this chapter, we'll cover practical tips on how to challenge your bright child in the classroom, after school and on weekends, and at home. However, all of these suggestions won't be entirely appropriate for every child. Only you know which activities and classroom modifications will interest your first grader. Try to imagine if your child would be intrigued and engaged by the different suggestions. If so, then do what you can to set it up. Sometimes all it takes is a little ingenuity to challenge even the brightest of children.

CLASSROOM SOLUTIONS

The first place to challenge your bright first grader is in the classroom. This becomes especially important when class sizes are large or there is a great disparity in skill levels. But, how do you help when you're not actually *in* the classroom? The answer's simple—talk with your child's teacher. This message bears repeating. There is nothing more important than getting to know your child's teacher. Together, you can figure out the best ways to keep your bright child challenged and interested in classroom activities. This will keep your child happy, stimulated, and engaged in learning. As mentioned earlier, it will also keep her out of trouble. Here are some effective ways to keep your brainy first grader from getting bored in her classroom:

Class Reading Club

Does your first grader adore reading? Are you willing to lend a helping hand? If so, you might want to talk with the teacher about creating a Class Reading Club. A reading club is similar to a book group, but it functions on a more basic level. Children check out books from the classroom, school, or local library. Once they are finished, they add the title and number of pages to a pre-made chart in the classroom. After the title, they check either the "thumbs up" or "thumbs down" box. Once a week, time is given in class to discuss the books of the week. Children are given the opportunity to describe their books to a friend and convince them to either read the book or skip it.

John Grady, a teacher in Chicago, IL, uses the Reading Club with a lot of success.

He says that he can count on the Reading Club to liven the class up and spark heated debate about which books are the "best" and "worst" of the week. Mr. Grady allows his students to read as many books as they like as long as they enter the information on the classroom chart. He rewards students with a pencil for every seventy-five pages read. Mr. Grady says that all of his students benefit from this program. His bright students especially love it because they have something concrete to do once they're done with their work. He also makes a point of tracking their progress to make sure they're challenging themselves to work at their highest level. For the lower achieving students and reluctant readers, he'll set goals with each student to encourage them. Needless to say, the children become very competitive with themselves to read, read, read.

How do you get a reading club going in your child's first grade classroom? Offer to help get it started. Talk with the teacher about what needs to be done to set up this easy-to-manage program. Sometimes all it takes is for you to make a poster-sized class chart with the students' names and book information listed along the top. Other times it can mean volunteering once a week to manage the program. These efforts will pay off when your child suddenly turns into a voracious reader.

Sometimes the job can be more difficult if the teacher does not have an adequate classroom library. However, you can always set up a mini-program at home using the techniques described above. You can reward your bright child accordingly and send the selected book to school for him to read quietly at his desk when he's finished working. When he's finished with a book, you can discuss why he gave it the thumbs up or thumbs down. The important thing is to keep your child reading. That is really the key to success in school and a great way to keep him busy and excited about learning.

Peer Tutoring

Sometimes the most practical solution turns out to be the most effective. Take peer tutoring, for instance. Peer tutoring is when two students are matched up to work together. One student is below grade level, and the other is typically above. They work together as a team—coaching, teaching, and helping each other out. Teachers often use peer tutoring in reading, but it's also useful for math, science, and other subjects.

Lisa Carron, a reading specialist in Norfolk, Virginia, once had a first grade student who was reading on a third grade level. He could finish his work in half the time of the other students. Once he finished the work, he would begin to flick erasers at the children around him. It didn't take long before Ms. Carron knew she had to do something with this bright but restless child. Her solution was to enlist him as a classroom helper. She paired him up with a child who was struggling to learn to read. He had a "Pass" to sit next to this child and help him as soon as his own work was completed. Both children benefited from this solution, and the behavior problem was soon extinguished.

The benefits can be substantial. The struggling student often gains confidence and skills while the more able child gets added practice and leadership skills (not to mention the satisfaction of helping out someone who needs it). Many research studies support the value of peer tutoring. Any one-on-one learning situation—whether adult-child or child-child—tends to results in achievement gains.

GATE — Gifted and Talented Programs

So, what do you do if you're convinced you've got a truly gifted child on your hands? There are Gifted and Talented Programs (GATE for short) available at a number of public schools across the country. However, it's sometimes difficult to get your child to qualify based on the number of requirements your local school district mandates. The first step is to know what "gifted" means and the signs to look for. Then talk with the teacher to see if your child is a good candidate for a GATE program.

In a nutshell, gifted and talented children show an outstanding ability in a variety of areas. Their giftedness can be demonstrated in general intellectual ability (IQ) or in more specific achievement abilities areas such as creativity (art, music, or the performing arts), leadership, or athletics. Gifted children are also thought to have highly developed abilities in these areas:

- ➤ Reading
- ➤ Literature
- ➤ Math reasoning
- ➤ Science
- ➤ The Arts
- ➤ Social Studies and Current Events

Gifted children also tend to have a lot of different hobbies and hold many interests. A gifted child may be an avid stamp collector while being an expert on dinosaurs. They also usually read more and gravitate toward more complex books than the average first grader. Games are also important to gifted children, and they like complicated, rule-dense, thinking kinds of games that challenge them on a number of levels. These traits tend to be evident early on, and they become more obvious with age.

With all this said, if you've got a gifted child on your hands, chances are, you've known for quite some time. Gifted children can be a handful, and they often demand complex answers and a variety of activities to keep them amused. This is precisely why a gifted child deserves special educational programs and services beyond those normally given by schools. These "special programs" will challenge and help gifted children to realize their potential talents.

Talk with your child's teacher to see if GATE programs or something similar are an option for your child. Some schools hire specially trained teachers to work with gifted students. Many times, gifted students are brought together for several hours a day to work together in a small group setting. If your school does not offer special services for gifted children, you may need to find additional after-school and weekend activities to keep your bright first grader from getting bored and restless in the regular educational program.

AFTER-SCHOOL ADVENTURES

Though what happens in the classroom is very important, there's also the matter of *after-school time*. The hours between the final bell and dinner can be an amazing block of time to develop new skills and interests. While we're not suggesting that you overdo it with an over-abundance of activity, we do suggest that after school can be an optimal time for your first grader. Based on our experience with children in the classroom as well as advice from the teachers we've interviewed, we've compiled a list of some fabulous ways to keep your first grader excited about learning.

Athletics

Youth Leagues

If your first grader has an excess of energy or could use some work with his coordination, why not try sports? Youth leagues are a terrific way to build physical skills like coordination and rhythm. They also have a sidebenefit of developing cooperation, sportsmanship, and a winning attitude. Also, they will help your child stay healthy and burn off some of that extra energy.

While most elementary schools don't have organized sports teams, there are plenty of other options for your first grader. A good place to start is by asking the school if there is an after-school sports program. If not, most communities have youth leagues for soccer, softball, basketball, flag football, or swimming. Call your local YMCA, or ask other parents for some resources.

Martial Arts

Judo, karate, tae kwon do, tai chi, and aikido are just a sampling of the martial arts that have become popular with boys and girls of all ages. The benefits of practicing these arts are often described as both mental and physical. Children build their strength and physical skills while concentrating on controlled and challenging movements. As the students progress through more difficult movements, they build more confidence and self-reliance.

One of the many good things about martial arts is that the philosophy behind them does not stress competition or violence. Instead, these Eastern sports emphasize self-improvement and harmony with the universe. Furthermore, the martial arts emphasize a code of respect—respect for the instructors as well as other students in the classroom—an invaluable lesson for people of any age.

The martial arts are particularly appropriate for a child who is lacking confidence or who is intimidated by competitive sports. They do require more concentration and control than, say, playing football, making them a perfect choice for bright children who need mental challenges along with physical activity. Some martial arts schools even provide educational lessons including anatomy, geography, and history to make a class even more intellectually stimulating. Check the yellow pages or ask other parents about local martial arts schools and programs.

Dance

The world of dance awaits your child. You'll be amazed at the variety of classes available: ballet, jazz, tap, and even African dance to live drumbeats. While styles of dance vary with their moves and choreography, they do offer many of the same benefits to kids. They teach concentration as new steps are learned and put into sequence, develop coordination skills, and help keep children in shape.

Ballet, jazz, and tap are still the champs when it comes to popularity. Young girls flock to ballet classes because of the princess-like quality of professional ballerinas. Ballet is a great way to learn posture, grace, self-discipline, and precision. Early tap and jazz classes also teach these skills in a child-friendly atmosphere with more upbeat music and opportunities for creative improvisation.

The type of dance your child chooses depends on her interests and particular skills. An ideal way to select a particular type of dance is to sit in on different classes to find the one that is most exciting for your child. You can also attend dance performances with your child to get a better sense of the various styles of dance out there.

The Arts

Arts & Crafts

Most first grade programs include at least a few hours a week of art class where it's common to find children painting, coloring, and making collages. This may be enough to satisfy the artistic needs of most children. But what do you do if you have a budding Picasso on your hands? There are plenty of children who seem to have been born knowing how to sketch, paint, or draw with more ability than most adults. If this sounds familiar, you might want to consider enrolling your child in an after-school art class. Classes in painting, drawing, printmaking, photography, papermaking, clay pottery, bookmaking, woodwork, and much, much more are available.

Most local museums, art councils, and cultural centers offer arts and crafts classes after school and on weekends. Ask other parents, call your local museum, do an Internet search, or read the newspaper's calendar section for offerings in your area.

Another option—albeit a more expensive one—is enrolling your child in a private art school. Students sometimes have the choice of joining a group of other students in a class or working one-on-one with the teacher in private lessons. These classes offer more intense and intricate art projects that intrigue even the most discriminating child artist.

A third idea is to seek out local artists who offer private lessons in their homes or studios. This is a more affordable way to have private lessons than enrollment in an art school. Again, ask other parents or neighbors if they know anyone who offers art lessons. You might be surprised at the number of available choices.

Museums

Museums aren't just for art anymore. There are loads of different kinds of museums—ones that explore natural history, science, different cultures, or even local folklore. Museums are a terrific learning resource as the topics are usually fascinating and the displays are very straightforward. Often, there may be a workshop or a film related to the display—check with the museum's schedule.

Contact your local chamber of commerce to find out what kinds of museums are located in your community. You and your child can learn so many new things from this shared adventure, and you'll have fun discussing your discoveries.

Acting Classes

If your child loves the spotlight, he may be a blossoming actor. If you encourage this interest, you may help your child in greater ways than you could imagine. Being in a play is an intellectual and artistic experience all in one. Memorizing lines will enhance memory skills. Learning cues will develop your child's sense of timing and spatial relations. Better yet, bringing an actual character to life will tap into your child's most creative resources.

Help your first grader develop this interest by finding ways to get him on stage. Some schools have drama clubs or a yearly theater production. Children's theater groups also put on major and minor productions. Talk to a drama teacher (one at your school or even another school) or try an Internet search for children's theater in your area.

Instrument Lessons

If your first grader is bursting with music—dancing and singing to every catchy tune, drumming out rhythms, or just possessing a great love for music—it might be time to think about music lessons. They will allow her to tap into her musical skills and help foster the dedication, precision, and tenacity that come with practicing a new instrument.

Some schools are fortunate enough to have the resources to offer music or instrument lessons; others are not. Even schools that offer these courses usually don't until the second or third grade. If your child has shown an interest in music before this time, there's no reason to wait. Learning to play an instrument involves many of the same skills as reading, learning a foreign language, and math, while channeling your child's creative energy.

Language Lessons

Learning a second language is a fabulous way to keep kids excited about learning, and it helps them to develop important learning skills. These *cognition skills* will help your child become a better student with more advanced thinking and reasoning skills.

If you speak a second language, begin by teaching your child simple words and phrases. Find out if she's interested in taking a more structured approach to learning the language. If so, there are many ways to get her involved. Quite a few community organizations offer small group language classes. The more traditional languages are French and Spanish, but many communities offer courses in Korean, Japanese, Yiddish, and other languages.

While language classes can be a great way to keep your child stimulated, it's important that they're child-friendly. A good children's program will be engaging, using techniques like arts and crafts, song, dance, theater, and outdoor activities to teach language in a lively way.

If you live near language schools, take advantage of the wonderful opportunities they afford. If not, keep on the lookout for special opportunities in the summer at camps and institutes.

AT-HOME EXPLORATIONS

There's no place like home to challenge your bright child. You have all the resources at your fingertips to create a challenging yet comfortable situation for him. No racing around, organizing carpools, or fighting traffic to keep your child interested in school. The answers can often be found in your kitchen cupboards or backyard. Below are some of our favorite ways to keep first graders active and busy at home.

At Home Art Projects

Origami

Origami, the Japanese art of folding colorful paper into shapes of animals and other objects, is an easy and exciting at-home project. Origami is also inexpensive and convenient. Most children need minimal guidance to learn it, and clean up is fast. Aside from just being "fun," Origami is also educational. Learning how to fold the paper into different shapes involves geometric thinking and problem solving. It often gives children a hands-on way to explore angles, shapes, and lines.

Origami kits are available in toy stores and on the Internet. They include everything you need to get started: instructions, colored tissue paper, and different ideas of shapes to make. If your child begins to love this hobby, there are books and kits available with more complicated ideas. But be prepared—if all goes well, paper birds, frogs, and insects might soon inhabit every inch of your house!

Make a game board

If your child is an avid drawer, you can use his artistic talents to draw or paint a game board. On a large poster board, you and your child can construct a maze that is a route from beginning to end with a square block representing each step. Use miniature toys as the game pieces, and let the roll of the dice move you forward. Your child can sprinkle visual rewards or pitfalls throughout the route (e.g.: "land on this square and move six spaces back").

An example of a specific game theme

"How does Jason get his new bike?"

- Use for example, a miniature shoe or car as the game pieces
- Draw picture of Jason on foot at the beginning, Jason on a bike at the end
- Sprinkle the route with related visual pitfalls (e.g. flat tires, broken seat) and rewards (e.g. new bell)
- Invite the whole family to play

Create a miniature art gallery

Let your child choose an original theme, create art works, then hang them up in an art gallery style. Choose any room in the house, and designate it as an art gallery. Flat art, such as paintings and drawings, can be glued to construction paper to give it a nice frame. Then you can hang it on the wall. 3-D objects, such as papier-mâché masks or mobiles, can be hung from the ceiling.

Your child may have a lot of ideas of his own for the art he wants to create, but if he is unsure of where to start, here are a few ideas:

- Family and self portraits
- Pictures of new species by mixing two different animals. For example, a zebra/bird or tiger/giraffe
- Drawings of what he sees out the different windows of your house

Fun Music Activity

If your child likes to sing or play an instrument, why not make her into your household recording star? All you need is a tape recorder and a quiet room. You can practice children's songs together and then tape them until you have an entire tape of songs. If you have other children that have other musical talents, bring them together to collaborate on fun and simple songs. Once the tape is done, you can play it at your leisure. This activity is guaranteed to send your first grader giggling and thrilled to hear herself played back.

Sharing Language Skills

If your child's talent lies in language, there are many ways to encourage second language acquisition at home. For starters, you can share your own language skills. Almost everyone knows a few words from another language. If you remember how to count to ten in Spanish, teach your child. Say *bon soir* instead of good-night. When you put her on the bus in the morning, exchange *adios*'s. Getting into the habit of using words from other languages will make her more comfortable speaking another tongue, and get her accustomed to the new sounds. She'll love sharing a "secret language" with you.

Another good ongoing exercise is the use of language labels. A common practice in American families hosting foreign exchange students is to label household items in English. Try this with a language other than English in your home. Children love knowing the double or even triple names for things. It can also make even the most ordinary exchanges *extraordinary*; instead of passing the salt, you'll be passing *das Salz*.

Better yet, if your native language is something other than English, why not teach your child some words and phrases? Children love learning different ways of saying things, especially if it's the language mom or dad grew up speaking. More importantly, however, sharing your own language will help you share an important part of your family history with your child. Your culture will be kept alive, and your child will feel closer to a part of you that was unknown before.

The Young Scientist

A Scientific Scrap Book

If your child is fascinated by nature, she can create a scientific scrapbook. The range of topics and locations is limitless. Together, you can go on nature walks collecting different kinds of leaves, flowers, and/or bugs then glue them in a book, writing down where they were found. Leave an empty page beside every item, and then go to the library or surf the Internet together to find the name and qualities of each collected thing. Have your child write the scientific and layman's name on the blank page, and then write qualities about it such as whether it's poisonous, in what seasons it's active, etc. on the opposing page. By the way, these nature walks don't have to take your far from home. A simple walk around the neighborhood or even the house may leave you with your hands full of scrapbook materials. This is a project where you'll both learn a thing or two, and you're guaranteed to have fun "leafing" through the book once it's done.

GREAT IDEA!

Quality Time and Communication with Mom and Dad

Sometimes your child's active mind needs to spend quiet time with mom and dad. With all of the hustle and bustle of day-to-day life, quiet time is often pushed aside and forgotten. Trust us—kids, especially first graders, like to spend time with their parents. Whether it's telling a story, reading at bedtime, exploring the neighborhood, or simple things like looking at the pictures in a *National Geographic* magazine together, there's nothing better than having mom or dad's undivided attention.

Keep this in mind when you make decisions about how to spend free time together. That often means turning on the answering machine, putting work aside, and saving the dinner cleanup until later. It may seem like it's impossible to find the time, but with some careful planning and prioritizing, it can be done. Perhaps a neighbor could take care of the other children while you take your child on an errand, just the two of you. That will give you plenty of time to talk—really talk—without interruptions.

The key aspect of quality time is *interaction*. This means talking with your child about the activity or adventure. Find out how he feels about it. Is he excited? Nervous? Happy? Find out the *why* behind his answers. For instance, if you're on a hike, take time to inspect the life around you. Listen to your child's observations and ask specific questions about them. Given the age of most first graders, concrete questions about specific things will generate the best responses. Ask which plant he likes the best. Or, allow him to lead the way along the trail.

At home, let him explain her school activities to you. Ask her about the science projects or social studies topics being covered. Your child will relish explaining things to you, and you can be fascinated by all the things he's learning.

The important thing is that you're spending special time with your child. You'll be working side by side to learn about the world around you whether it's outdoors or in your family room. This quality time will mean the world to your child, not to mention helping her learn from the person who knows her best—you!

One More Thought . . . A Healthy Schedule

All too often, parents with the best intentions overload their children with too many extracurricular activities. While all of the ideas offered will allow your child to develop additional skills and interests, they are only useful if they're *fun*. In other words, if your child feels stressed or burdened with his schedule, then they will be of no use to him. If a child is carted from hockey to violin lessons to acting class, he will soon grow weary of all of them.

Moderation is the key. It's important to keep in mind that you're dealing with a six- or seven-year-old child. You're not out to produce an Olympic athlete or get accepted at an Ivy League school. Well, at least not now.

Allow your first grader the chance to be a kid. That means scheduling a couple of extra activities that are interesting to him. The schedule will also be more manageable for you and your family and your child will look forward to attending them. Then, and only then, will the activities provide the intellectual stimulation and enrichment he's yearning for.

The Best Stuff
for First Graders

Okay, you've learned everything you could ever want to know about your first grader, so now what? Where does a parent go from here?

We have taken the next step and included the best books, magazines, web sites, and software for kids. Many included below are considered "edutainment." Simply put, your child will be learning something and having fun at the same time.

BOOKS

Here is a list of books that are award winners or that come highly recommended by educators. If you don't find what you like here, follow the instructions below for further assistance.

If we were to list all the quality children's books out there, they'd take up at least half of this book. Just stop by your local children's bookstore, and you'll be lost for hours in the wonderful tales and enchanting illustrations that inhabit so many of them. If you need a reminder of how important it is to expose your first grader to books, just think back to the first time you fell in love with a book. It's almost a magical experience! For children who are just learning to read, a good book can represent a liberation of the imagination that is unparalleled.

The U.S. Department of Education has offered the following tips for finding the right books for you and your children to enjoy.

Look For Books

The main thing is to find books you both love. They will shape your child's first impression of the world of reading.

What To Do

1. Ask friends, neighbors, and teachers to share the names of their favorite books.

2. Visit your local public library, and as early as possible, get your child a library card. Ask the librarian for help in selecting books. (Also see the resources section at the end of this book.)

3. Look for award-winning books. Each year the American Library Association selects children's books for the Caldecott Medal for illustration and the Newberry Medal for writing.

4. Check the book review sections of newspapers and magazines for recommended new children's books.

5. As soon as they're old enough, have your children join you in browsing for books and making selections.

6. If you and your child don't enjoy reading a particular book, put it aside and pick up another one.

Keep in mind your child's reading level and listening level are different. When you read easy books, beginning readers will soon be reading along with you. When you read more advanced books, you will instill a love of stories, and you will build the motivation that transforms children into lifelong readers.

The list we've compiled is a mix of age-old classics and successful newcomers. Which books you choose for your child's library will depend on his individual tastes and preferences. A trip with your child in the local bookstore or library would be an ideal place to start.

Picture Books and Easy Readers

And If the Moon Could Talk, by Kate Banks (Farrar, Straus & Giroux)

Are You My Mother?, by P. D. Eastman (Random House, 1988)

Bark, George, by Jules Fieffer (HarperCollins, 1999)

Bedtime for Frances, by Russell Hoban (HarperCollins Juvenile Books, 1995)

Cloudy with a Chance of Meatballs, by J. Barrett (Aladdin Paperbacks, 1982)

The Complete Adventures of Curious George, by Margaret Rey and H. A. Rey (Houghton Mifflin Co, 1995)

The Complete Tales of Winnie the Pooh, by A. A. Milne (Penguin USA, 1996)

Eloise, by Kay Thompson (Simon & Schuster, 1969)

The Gardener, by Sarah Stewart and David Small (Farrar, Straus & Giroux, 1997)

Ice Cream Larry, by Jill Pinkwater and Daniel M. Pinkwater (Marshall Cavendish, 1999)

If You Give a Pig a Pancake, by Laura Joffe Numeroff (HarperCollins Juvenile Books, 1998)

Lyle, Lyle, Crocodile, by Bernard Waber (Houghton Mifflin Co, 1987)

The Velveteen Rabbit, by Margery Williams (Doubleday, 1958)

Books by Subject

These books are great for encouraging your child to learn more about her favorite subject or to find a fun way to learn about a subject that might give her trouble. Children need to understand that the classroom is not the only place they can learn, and books are a great way to accomplish that lesson.

English/Language Arts
Emily [Emily Dickinson, Poet], by Michael Bedard (Doubleday 1992)
Author: A True Story, by Helen Lester (Houghton Mifflin, 1997)

Math
Give Me Half, by Stuart J. Murphy (Harper Trophy, 1996)
Eating Fractions, by Bruce McMillan (Scholastic, 1991)

Science
Balloons and Other Fun Things; Gravity; Seeds and How They Grow; In the Pool, by Richard Scarry (Simon Spotlight, 1998)
Life in the Rainforest: Plants, Animals, and People, by Melvin Berger, et al. (Ideals Childrens Books, 1994)

Social Studies
Me on the Map, by Joan Sweeney (Dragonfly, 1998)
The Children's Book of Heroes, by William J. Bennet, editor (Simon & Schuster, 1997)

Computers
Scholastic's The Magic School Bus Gets Programmed: A Book About Computers, by Nancy White et al. (Scholastic, 1999)
My First Book About the Internet, by Sharon Cromwell (Troll, 1997)

Music
The Reader's Digest Children's Songbook/Lyric Booklet (Reader's Digest, 1985)
Meet the Orchestra, by Ann Hayes (Harcourt Brace, 1995)

Social Skills/Manners
The Meanest Thing to Say: Little Bill Books for Beginning Readers, by Bill Cosby (Cartwheel, 1997)
Perfect Pigs: An Introduction to Manners, by Marc Tolon Brown (Little Brown & Co, 1983)

Magazines

The following list of magazine cover a variety of topics and reading levels. Included is a synopsis of content.

Chickadee Magazine, how-to, personal experience.

Children's Playmate, articles with health, sports, fitness, and nutrition themes

Crayola Kids Magazine, crafts, puzzles, and activities (See also websites)

Highlights for Children, unusual, meaningful stories appealing to both boys and girls

Hopscotch, The Magazine for Girls, covers pets, crafts, hobbies, games, science, fiction, history, and puzzles

Jack and Jill, articles, stories, and activities with health, safety, exercise, and nutrition themes

Owl Magazine, The Discovery Magazine for Children, personal experience, photo features, science, and environmental features

Ranger Rick, articles relating to nature, conservation, the outdoors, environmental problems, or natural science

Sports Illustrated For Kids, games, general interest, humor, how-to, photos, inspirational

Time for Kids, current events, photos (See also websites)

U.S. Kids, A Weekly Reader Magazine, general interest, how-to, interview, science, computers, multiculturalism

CHILDREN'S WEBSITES*

Regarding Website Content

Parents should always supervise their children while on the Internet. While the sites listed below have excellent standards for content, there are sites on the Internet which have no standards for content. This should not deter parents from encouraging their child to spend time on the Web. As evidenced by the sites we have listed below, your child will have the resources to learn about anything that might interest her. Follow the simple rules below, and your time on the Internet will be time well spent.

* At the time of publication, the websites listed here were current. Due to the ever-changing nature of the Web, we cannot guarantee their continued existence or content.

BellSouth Online offers these helpful lessons to teach your child about Internet safety. As well as helpful hints to teach her about the Internet.

➤ Don't give out personal information such as your name, address, or phone number
➤ Do tell a parent or teacher about new friends found on the internet
➤ Don't believe everything you read online
➤ Don't give out your password
➤ Do tell an adult if something or someone makes you feel bad or uncomfortable

If you have concerns and you would like to know more about Internet safety, try looking at the FBI's site, "A Parent's Guide to Internet Safety," at *www.fbi.gov/library/pguide/pguide.htm* or you can try *www.ed.gov/pubs/parents/internet* for "Parents Guide to the Internet" which is hosted by the U.S. Department of Education.

Reference Guides

http://kids.infoplease.com
At infoplease, students not only have access to a homework center, but also to almanacs, dictionaries, and encyclopedias.

www.brittanica.com
This site offers free access to the Encylopedia Britannica!

www.wordcentral.com
Merriam-Webster's site encourages children to build their vocabulary using an online dictionary. It also offers "Daily Buzzwords" and games for children.

www.pathfinder.com/TFK/
TIME for Kids, the online answer to the magazine, offers articles on current events. "News Scoop" offers stories customized for second and third graders.

Edutainment

www.crayola.com

The people at Crayola offer a site full of crafts for kids. There is a game room, coloring books, craft suggestions, and stories.

www.exploratorium.edu

The famous San Francisco museum by the same name hosts this site. The museum is dedicated to science, art, and human perception. Here you will find exhibitions from the museum, activities, and resources for projects. Check it out!

www.funschool.com

Funschool promises regularly updated educational content for children. Click on "First Grade" from the homepage for content developed especially for your child.

www.geocities.com/EnchantedForest/Tower/1217/grade1.html

This site is aptly titled "First Grade Backpack." Great stories to read, interesting places, awesome animals, fantastic arithmetic, and holiday fun are just a few of the pages to visit.

http://kids.msfc.nasa.gov

NASA is sure to find some new recruits for the space program from this site! Complete with space art, space stories, and games, this site will keep children captivated for hours.

www.nick.com

This site comes from the folks at Nickelodeon. While much of this site is dedicated to their programming, there are other pages that offer more of a challenge. Go to "Noggin" from the home page to find games and fun facts for children.

http://nyelabs.kcts.org

A must for the budding scientist! Bill Nye, The Science Guy, has created a site that is a lot of fun for kids. It is loaded with interesting facts and lots of safe science projects to do at home.

www.pbs.org

PBS has a great site for kids, parents, and teachers alike. Head to PBS KIDS from the home page and be astonished by the quality and quantity of content. There are no shortages of great pages from *Sesame Street*, *Zoom*, and *Arthur*. Colorful and filled with all your favorite characters, this site is a MUST for parents and kids.

www.snoopy.com
The official Peanuts website makes learning fun for children. There are comic strips, but this site includes games and activities for first graders.

www.worldbook.com
Head straight for World Book's Fun and Learning page. There you will find games, news, and even a Cyber Camp complete with a summer's worth of activities.

www.yahooligans.com
From the creators of Yahoo comes Yahooligans, a web guide designed for children. Topics included are sports, around the world, and arts and entertainment.

SOFTWARE/CD-ROMS

If you want your child to feel comfortable using a computer, but you aren't sure you feel comfortable having them go online, software is a safe and effective alternative. These programs are easy enough for your child to use, and they are not only learning how to use the computer but also math and reading skills.

Keep in mind, these activities on the computer are better than TV and cost less than most video games!

Reading and Math

Curious George Reads, Writes & Spells for Grades 1 & 2
Curious George is a timeless classic who has made a seamless entry into the world of computers. There are twelve activities that follow George through yet another misadventure. As an added bonus, there are thirty pages that can be printed out for your child. A great value at $19.99!

Disney's Math Quest with Aladdin Ages 6-9
This software offers three skill levels and eighteen activities. Students use math to complete Aladdin's adventure and then

receive a certificate of achievement to keep them motivated to learn. Cost: $14.99

Logical Journey of the Zoombinis

Teachers have assured us that problem solving and thinking skills are crucial to a child's development. This software helps foster these skills. While it may be challenging to first graders, it is a program they will definitely grow into. Cost: $14.99

My Personal Tutor 1st & 2nd Grade

At $34.95, this is a great value. This software features animated adventures that offer plenty of opportunities for children to improve their math *and* reading skills.

Madeline 1st & 2nd Grade Reading

Featuring Madeline, the lovable French student, this software will build and improve reading skills in your six-to-nine-year-old. There are forty-five multilevel activities all led by Madeline. Cost: $34.95 (If you love this program, try Madeline 1st & 2nd Grade Math.)

Science

Dinosaur Adventure 3-D

At $19.99 this is a value! This has state-of-the-art animation featured in seven games and twenty-five movies. There is a workbook that can be printed from the software that assesses critical thinking and creativity skills.

Magic School Bus 1.0 Solar System

This program not only offers real videos from NASA but also allows your child to travel through space. There are also great interactive experiments. Cost: $14.99

Social Studies

My First Amazing World Explorer and History Explorer

This program features time travel through eight different historical periods as well as sixteen different videos. It's great way to make history come alive! Cost: $19.99

Road Adventures U.S.A.

This is a great program for reinforcing geography and planning. Students can plan a trip and explore famous landmarks from the safety and comfort of home. Great for rainy days too! Cost: $26.99

Foreign Language

Rosetta Stone: Spanish Explorer Ages 6 and Up

This is intended to be interactive. It requires user response. Users can determine their own learning styles and customize their lessons. Includes 800 real-life color pictures and the skill of native speakers. This program is also available in everything from French to Swahili. Cost: $19.99

Art

Crayola Creativity Pack Print Factory and Make a Masterpiece

This software offers plenty of tools to draw, paint, and color. There are also reading and writing activities. Cost: $29.99 for both programs

Sesame Street Music Maker

Sesame Street has its bases covered with this program. Your child can sing and dance in the karaoke lounge or make music with eight different activities. It also includes samples of music from around the world. Cost: $19.99

Just For Fun

My Disney Kitchen

Your child can decorate the kitchen and proceed to put it to use. There are thirty videos, and Mickey and Minnie are on hand to taste the recipes with which your child experiments. It's great for creativity, and kids can make a mess of this kitchen with no cleanup. Cost: $14.99

Tonka Construction 2

This is a great disc for the aspiring architect/builder in your family! This program offers users the opportunity to create their own buildings and the challenge of finding the way to tear down old buildings. It has plenty of fun challenges for kids! Cost $29.99

Timon & Pumbaa Adventures in Typing

If you really want to give your child a head start in computers, you can also check out this CD-ROM. With the help of the lovable Lion King characters, your child can learn the basics of typing. Finger placement, homerow technique, and letter recognition are taught through games and activities. Cost: $14.99

REMEMBER: When purchasing software, make sure that it is compatible with the computer you have at home.

WEBSITES FOR PARENTS

As you can probably tell from the suggestions in the trouble shooting section found at the end of each chapter, the Internet is a great resource for parents to find helpful hints or even just to vent your ideas and frustrations. Below are some of the best sites for parents who want help or to blow off steam.

www.about.com

While you may use this site for anything about which you might want to learn, it has particularly strong links and articles on parenting and education. Your about.com expert has no shortage of information and helpful ideas.

http://cluser1.bellsouthlonline.com/comcalendar/education/ bscomm_edu_llls_parents.html

It may seem strange that BellSouth would have a web site on education, but it does, and it is terrific! This site has plenty of parent-friendly suggestions and tips on helping your grade-schooler to be her best.

www.ed.gov

Your tax dollars are at work! This site is run by The U.S. Department of Education. From the page listed above, parents can find out information on activities for children, the Internet, family involvement in education and early childhood education. The site offers a seemingly endless supply of *excellent* resources.

www.escore.com

Escore.com is a leading online resource to help parents play an active role in their child's learning and development. This site includes tips for parents and educational products for children.

www.familyeducation.com

This is a wonderful all-around site. It offers information on your child's development through the years, family activities, family news and topics, tips and resources to help you in your parenting, software downloads, message boards, ideas from parents, and advice from familyeducation.com experts. What more could you need?

www.helpforfamilies.com

Helpforfamilies.com was developed by a clinical psychologist striving to help parents help their children. This site has several useful topics in dealing with children.

www.homeworkcentral.com

This site has excellent resources for teachers, students, and parents. Links are provided to helpful articles and worksheets that parents can use to help their children.

www.lightspan.com

What a great site! Lightspan offers plenty of information on education and parenting issues. The site is divided by grade level, so you can track your child's progress through the years. This comprehensive site also offers great information not only for parents but also for teachers and children.

www.parentsjournal.org

This site offers resources for parents dealing with problem situations with their child. The contributors to this site are teachers and parents which means that the information is developed from relevant experience.

www.shearwater-boats.com/improvingeducation.org

This site has lots of articles and resources for parents to help their child learn. The worksheet generator is a bonus for parents who want to help their child improve his skills at home.

www.teachingtips.com
This site was a great resource in researching this book. Anna Gregory has a great site backed up by years of experience in the classroom. Go to her with your questions!

AND MORE BOOKS

Activity Books Parents Can Give to Their Children

101 Fresh & Fun Critical Thinking Activities: Engaging Activities and Reproducibles to Develop Kids' Higher-Level Learning (Scholastic, 1998)
Big First Grade Workbook, by Schoolzone Publishing (Schoolzone, 1997)
Grade Boosters: First Grade Reading, by Faybeth Harter (Lowell House, 1996)
Grade Boosters: First Grade Vocabulary, by Vicky Shiotsu (Lowell House, 1999)
Grade Boosters: First Grade Math, by Zondra Lewis Knapp (Lowell House, 1997)

For Further Reading

If you find that these books and sites still don't have what you are looking for, the following list of books may help you get some answers.

What Your First Grader Needs to Know: Fundamentals of a Good First Grade Education, E. D. Hirsch, Jr., editor (Dell Publishing, 1998)
Helping Your Child to Learn: A Proven System That Shows Parents How to Help Their Children Study and Receive Top Grades in Elementary and Junior High, by Gordon W. Green, Jr. (Carol, 1994)
101 Educational Conversations With Your Kindergartner-1st Grader, by Vito Peronne (Chelsea House, 1993)
The School Savvy Parent: 365 Insider Tips to Help You Help Your Child, by Rosemarie Clark (Free Spirit, 1999)
365 Fun-Filled Learning Activities You Can Do With Your Child, by Mary S. Weaver (Adams Media, 1999)